Hindu Wisdom
for All God's Children

FAITH MEETS FAITH
An Orbis Series in Interreligious Dialogue
Paul F. Knitter, General Editor

Editorial Advisors
Julia Ching
Diana Eck
Karl-Josef Kuschel
Lamin Sanneh
George E. Tinker
Felix Wilfred

In the contemporary world, the many religions and spiritualities stand in need of greater communication and cooperation. More than ever before, they must speak to, learn from, and work with each other in order both to maintain their vital identities and to contribute to fashioning a better world.

FAITH MEETS FAITH seeks to promote interreligious dialogue by providing an open forum for exchanges among followers of different religious paths. While the series wants to encourage creative and bold responses to questions arising from contemporary appreciations of religious plurality, it also recognizes the multiplicity of basic perspectives concerning the methods and content of interreligious dialogue.

Although rooted in a Christian and Maryknoll theological perspective, the series does not endorse any single school of thought or approach. By making available to both the scholarly community and the general public works that represent a variety of religious and methodological viewpoints, FAITH MEETS FAITH seeks to foster an encounter among followers of the religions of the world on matters of common concern.

FAITH MEETS FAITH SERIES

Hindu Wisdom
for All God's Children

Francis X. Clooney, S.J.

ORBIS BOOKS

Maryknoll, New York 10545

The Catholic Foreign Mission Society of America (Maryknoll) recruits and trains people for overseas missionary service. Through Orbis Books, Maryknoll aims to foster the international dialogue that is essential to mission. The books published, however, reflect the opinions of their authors and are not meant to represent the official position of the society.

Permission to reprint the following copyrighted material is gratefully acknowledged: to the Advaita Ashrama, Calcutta, for verses from Shankaracharya's *Vivekacudamani,* translated by Swami Madhavananda; to Oxford University Press for "Pied Beauty" and "Blessed Virgin Compared to Air We Breathe" from the *Poems of Gerard Manley Hopkins* (1985); to Penguin UK for selections from *Hindu Myths,* translated by Wendy Doniger O'Flaherty, reproduced by permission of Frederick Warne & Co. (1975); to the Feminist Press at the City University of New York for selections from "The Wet Nurse" in *Truth Tales* (1990); to Routledge for selections from "Draupadi" by Mahasweta Devi in *In Other Worlds* (1988); to the State University of New York Press for material from *Antal's Path of Love* by Vidya Dehejia (1990); to the Theosophical Publishing House, Adyar, Madras, India, for materials from *Saundarya Lahari,* translated by Pandit Subrahmanya Sastri and T. R. S. Ayyangar, and for diagrams from this work used in chapter 6 (1992); to Bantam Books, a division of Bantam, Doubleday, Dell Publishing Group, for selections from *Bhagavad-Gita* by Barbara Stoler Miller, translation copyright © 1986 by Barbara Stoler Miller; to Dover Publications, Inc.; for selections from Mohandas K. Gandhi, *The Story of My Life* (1983); to Yale University Press for selections from E. W. Burlingame, *Buddhist Parables* (1922); to the National Council of Churches of Christ in the USA for Biblical citations, all of which are taken from the *New Oxford Annotated Bible* published by Oxford University Press (1991).

Manufactured in the United States of America

Library of Congress Cataloging-in-Publication Data

Clooney, Francis Xavier, 1950-
    Hindu wisdom for all God's children / Francis X. Clooney.
      p. cm. – (Faith meets faith series)
    Includes index.
    ISBN 1-57075-164-1
    1. Hinduism – Doctrines.   I. Title.   II. Series: Faith meets
faith.
BL1212.72.C57   1998
294.5 – dc21   97-49195
                                            CIP

To
Irene H. Clooney and James J. Clooney
whose wisdom I encountered first

Contents

Introduction

When I was a junior in college and still early in my studies to become a Jesuit priest, I went to a conference on the international work of Jesuits. The main speaker was a respected Jesuit from the Philippines, Fr. Horatio de la Costa. In the course of his reflections he said that in today's world we are called to have "hearts as large as the world"; we need to imagine, think, empathize, pray across all the geographical and psychological distances and barriers which divide our world into parts. I had already been curious about the wider world, but the call to open our hearts gave new energy to my awakening interest, made it come alive in a concrete way. It was the right advice at the right time, and it opened a new pathway for me. I realized that I wanted to understand and experience the world, particularly its religious traditions, more fully and inclusively than I had until that time in my life. His simple words invited me to begin that spiritual quest.

When I graduated from college I was expected to teach high school for several years as part of my Jesuit training, so I started exploring opportunities outside the United States. I asked around and corresponded with Jesuits in different parts of the world. But I was most fascinated by the idea of going to India. Although I knew almost nothing about Hinduism or Buddhism, I did know that my heroes included Mohandas Gandhi and Mother Teresa. These two very different figures drew my attention to India; they made it seem a place where a person could live among the poor and learn from them in an intensely spiritual environment. Various factors made teaching in India impossible, so I took some good advice and wrote to the American Jesuits in Kathmandu, Nepal. I finally agreed to go there and teach at St. Xavier's School, which had been founded in Kathmandu in the early 1950s at the invitation of the king of Nepal.

Kathmandu, high in the Himalayas, is a place of spectacular beauty. The temples are so ancient you might take them as museums, except that they are still visited daily. Hindus and Buddhists live side by side, and since the Chinese conquest of Tibet in the 1950s, Tibetan monasteries too have become features of the landscape. If you stand in the right place, you can see Mount Everest from the roof of our school. It was a good setting for lofty religious expectations, a way of life where heart and mind could explore their own limits and yet nourish one another too. After the usual initial period of adjustment, the new and different quickly became ordinary; for the most part I was immersed in the everyday life of a boarding school, learning such diverse skills as how to teach Nepali boys to pronounce English properly, how to read classics such as *Julius Caesar* and *A Tale of Two Cities,* how to referee a soccer match, how to run a film projector, how to sleep under a mosquito net in the corner of a dormitory. I was with Hindu and Buddhist boys from 6:00 A.M., when I rang the bell to wake them up, to 9:30 P.M., when I hoped they would go to sleep. I learned to speak a bit of Nepali and how to read it in its Nagari script; I was introduced to the basics of local etiquette, the hows and whys of being a vegetarian (because of a respect for life, because the poor do not eat meat), the festivals of the Hindu and Buddhist calendars. I remember vividly leading a group of students at 4:00 A.M. one February morning to the great Shiva temple at Pashupati, so they could celebrate Shivaratri, Shiva's Night; I cannot forget spending several days at a Buddhist monastery in the hills, far off the beaten path. I explored daily devotions and routine pieties, temples and processions and festivals; I became very curious about the weekly animal sacrifices to the Goddess Durga (Kali) at a famous temple at Dakshin Kali, just south of the Kathmandu Valley. At times I felt a million miles from anywhere I had ever been before; at other times I felt entirely at home.

Because I had to teach "Moral Science" to ninth graders, I turned to what I thought would communicate religious and moral values concretely to my students, the stories of the gods and heroes of the Hindu tradition. I studied the *Bhagavad Gita* for the first time. I read and told stories of the Buddha's life and deeds and teachings, and recounted his simple acts of compassion and love. I found this verse which echoed what Fr. de la Costa had said about opening one's heart:

> As a mother with her life will guard her child, her only child,
> let my followers extend unboundedly their hearts to every living being.
> With love for all the world let them extend their hearts unboundedly,
> above, below, around, unchecked,
> with no ill will or hate, whether they stand, or sit, or walk, or rest.
> May my followers always pursue this mindfulness.[1]

---

1. From the *Sutta Nipata* I.8, as quoted in *The Life of the Buddha according to the Pali Canon,* as compiled and translated by Bhikku Nanamoli (Kandy: Buddhist Publication Society, 1978), 181.

I was learning how to teach and listen too, and with my students I was learning what was important and true for all of us, despite our different backgrounds. We went on retreats together, read local religious stories along with the New Testament, listened to devotional hymns along with popular American songs from the 1960s. I set up a prayer room in the school, which the boys adorned with images of the gods Krishna and Rama, Sarasvati the Goddess of wisdom, and the Buddha. That prayer room was a holy place, filled with the fragrance of fine bright powders and incense and so many fresh flowers, alive with songs the boys had learned from their parents and grandparents. I was deeply impressed then, and still am, by how fervently they sang of Lord Rama and his wife, Sita, how they simply placed themselves with this divine couple, at their feet. By their devotion, the boys helped me to pray, to find God right there, then, with them and never thereafter in the way I had before. I was being introduced to a wisdom beyond my expectations, and when I came home I was a better Catholic because of the experience. I traveled and learned, I began to see my tradition, my faith, and myself in a new light. I had encountered new wisdom, and maybe was a little wiser myself.

More than twenty years have passed since that first visit to a Hindu and Buddhist culture. After I was ordained a Catholic priest in 1978, I went to graduate school at the University of Chicago and studied the Hindu intellectual and religious traditions in detail; this gave me more occasions to spend long periods of time in India, mostly in the great city of Madras (now Chennai) in the south. I have learned many things from the Hindu religious traditions, but all that I have learned confirms my initial intuition as to how worthwhile and important it is to draw upon the wisdom of the religious traditions of India.

Hindu Wisdom for All God's Children is an effort to share what I have learned, in a way that makes it possible for readers to see for themselves and to explore their own experience in the mirror of Hindu wisdom. It is not a book by a specialist for specialists. I do not suppose that my readers are experts in Indian thought, nor even that they have any background knowledge of India, though I hope it will also be interesting to readers who have been to India or encountered Hindu wisdom in some way or another. I myself might be called an expert on just one or two of the topics that I raise in these chapters. I have read in their original languages some of the texts I discuss, and some I have read first or only in translation. At times I draw conclusions and make applications that might seem puzzling to people who have grown up Hindu or to some scholars in specific fields.

Hindu Wisdom is not the last word on anything, for it is simply meant to open up some possibilities, pathways an interested reader might travel in beginning to learn from India. Because the book is meant to aid the reader in beginning an intellectual and spiritual quest, its chapters offer specific instances with which the reader can look into something new, and then back into his or her own self — at new images of the divine, and then back into his or her own understanding of God. Though opportunities for fruitful comparison abound, only occasionally do I offer actual comparisons with religious traditions other than the Hindu, and most of these are from the Bible. Of course, since I am Roman Catholic and write from that background, everything I say may seem very Christian and Catholic at its roots. But that should be no problem if it is recognized and kept in mind; after all, we all have to start somewhere. Readers may eventually find their own, personally better ways to encounter Hindu wisdom, to study it, to present it to others, and some may even go to India themselves, to observe how all this works out at the beginning of the twenty-first century. My hope is that in the end all readers will strike out on their own and then encounter and integrate wisdom ever more widely, and from still other religious traditions.

"Hindu wisdom" points to many insights and ideas and experiences that are interwoven and layered, to be sampled in parts and then all at once too. There are many gods and goddesses, numerous widespread and local traditions, beliefs that are very ancient alongside beliefs seemingly as recent as yesterday. There are innumerable religious practices, ranging from some that attract us as wise and natural, to others that seem unfamiliar and so very foreign; there are many great saints, but they turn out to be very diverse, of every creed and spiritual path, and sometimes seemingly contradictory in terms of the wisdom they recommend. My experience has taught me that learning from the wisdom of Hinduism is very worthwhile — but which Hinduism do I mean? Some scholars vehemently refuse to use words like "Hinduism" or "Hindu wisdom" at all, saying that it is unfair to gather diverse materials and label them with such vague words. To a large extent they are correct, and their hesitations are appropriate. But the words "Hinduism" and "Hindu" remain useful in a book like this, perhaps necessary, as long as we also admit that the traditions we group under such labels are more rich and diverse than the ways in which we might fix them.

It is true that we can begin anywhere and simply enjoy the diversity, learning as we can and choose to learn, and eventually we will be drawn into the whole. Still, we must begin in some particular place or places — where? When I agreed to give the Tuohy Lectures at John Carroll University in the fall of 1996 and thereafter started to write a book based on those lectures, I had to make some decisions about where it is fruitful to begin learning about India. I have favored elements that are representative of some of the major strands within Hindu thought; I drew on the Sanskrit, Pali, Tamil, Bengali, and Gujarati language traditions; I reviewed basic creation myths and meditational practices, texts as well known as the *Bhagavad Gita* and Mohandas Gandhi's autobiography, others as rare as the *Pashupata Sutras* (a manual for ascetics) and the *Ocean of Beauty* (a guide to Goddess worship). On the whole, I have favored texts and themes which have been personally helpful to me, and I hope my readers will find them so.

Chapter 1 opens our exploration by reflecting on creation, creativity, and the beginnings of self-awareness, all in light of a Hindu creation myth. Since this chapter is a guide to all that follows, it is probably best read first *and* last. The six chapters that follow introduce six themes and ways of thinking religiously, in light of the Hindu traditions. Chapter 2 presents a philosophical tale of the discovery of the self and highlights one of the most famous strands of Hindu thought, the nondualist Vedanta, which held that ultimately there really is only one self for all reality. Chapter 3 focuses on the Buddha's telling his own story, how his journey to the forest and search of the past taught him to be at peace here and now. (By including the Buddha, I must add, I do not intend to present him as a Hindu, but rather to emphasize his role in the development of Indian wisdom and his importance to an understanding of Hinduism.) Chapter 4 turns us toward the desire for God and the quest to see God face to face, as this works out in the tradition of devotion to Krishna. Chapter 5 highlights the paradoxical nature of our encounter with God in the mystery of Shiva. Chapter 6 points to the totalization of human awareness and religious experience in Goddess worship, and in one particular strand of worship of the great Goddess. Chapter 7 brings our reflection on Hindu wisdom into the twentieth century by tracing how Mohandas Gandhi and the writer Mahasweta Devi describe authentic ways of being human in the modern world.

I regret that I could not include more. I have left out many aspects of Hindu wisdom; I pass over the *Ramayana* tradition, the poetry of Kabir, and most of the impressive achievements of the great philosophical and theological traditions. I say little about ritual performance, yogic practice, temple worship, processions and pilgrimages. For the most part I treat Hindu wisdom as a world unto itself. I introduce the Buddha, but without saying anything more about India's rich Buddhist traditions; I have nothing to say about other ascetical religions such as Jainism. I overlook the rich contributions to Indian culture and religion, and therefore to Hindu India too, made by Islam, Sikhism, and Christianity. I say nothing about the flourishing of Hinduism outside of India in ancient times, and now in the West. But these omissions are certainly not meant to deny the importance of these themes and traditions; I have tried to include important and interesting materials, but this does not mean that the wisdom I have omitted is unimportant or uninteresting!

Of course, some readers may decide that I have included too much. This sampling of Hindu wisdom may seem a bit too diverse for some tastes, and some readers may want to discover a unity underlying it all. It may help such readers to remember that many Hindus today accept the idea — an old one but perhaps never before so widespread — that there is only one divine reality manifest in innumerable forms and called by innumerable names. If you look deep enough, everything comes together. For me, though, it has always been the diversity and complexity of the divine in India that have helped me to think and imagine and pray differently, and it is better to read without worrying too soon about making everything fit together nicely.

The book originated as the six Walter and Mary Tuohy Lectures I gave at John Carroll University in the fall of 1996. Chapter 2 was later added to fill out a bit this introduction to the multifaceted traditions of Hindu wisdom. I am grateful to my hosts at John Carroll University, especially Professor Paul Lauritzen, coordinator for the Tuohy Chair, and the members and staff of the Religious Studies Department. The Jesuit community at John Carroll was also very gracious during my stay at the university. The response I received to the lectures themselves was both gratifying and informative, and I learned a great deal from my listeners. I likewise appreciate the hospitality of the Jesuit School of Theology in Berkeley, where I taught in the spring of 1997 while finishing the project of making the lectures into a book. I am particularly indebted to those who took the time to read drafts of my manuscript. Sr. Elizabeth Hillis of the Carmel of the Holy Family in Cleveland Heights, Ohio, gave me invaluable advice as I was turning the lectures into chapters. In the fall of 1997 my students at Boston College read the manuscript and gave me some valuable suggestions. Several friends were willing to read the full manuscript of the book and give me detailed comments: at John Carroll University, Professors Paul Nietupski and Maryclare Moroney; Christopher Meehan, an undergraduate who was already a veteran of time well spent in India; in Boston, Elizabeth Amrien, and at Boston College, Joseph Molleur (Ph.D. Cand. in Theology); my Hindu friends, Pravrajika Vrajaprana from the Sarada Convent in Montecito, California, and Prof. Anantanand Rambachan of St. Olaf's College in Minnesota; last but not least, my father, James J. Clooney, who has often expressed the hope that I write a book unencumbered by the learned details of Indology and theology. I am very pleased to dedicate this book to him and my mother, Irene H. Clooney. After all, wisdom begins at home.

1

In the Beginning

When I first arrived in Kathmandu, which I had thought to be very exotic, I remember being let down: things weren't as different as I had expected. People were people, I was still myself; the sun still rose in the East, set in the West. After a while I began to appreciate the commonplace continuities of everyday human living, and I began to recognize how much I had in common with the people, their traditions, their beliefs and practices. I had never been in Kathmandu before, but in some way I was right at home. I was obviously a foreigner, I could never quite fit in, yet here I could begin to see myself in a way I had never done before. When I returned to the United States two years later, I found America a bit strange too. I had started learning what it means to lose and find oneself again and again.

To be able to discover ourselves anew seems very important as we begin to learn from Hindu wisdom; to do this well, we need to reflect on what it even means to begin an intellectual and spiritual quest, and who we are that begin it. If we read reflectively with an eye toward what we are really doing as we read, we will be better able to enrich our thinking and living with Hindu wisdom. This first chapter therefore takes us back to the beginning — the beginning of our learning and the beginning of the world. As such, it is really a guide to the six chapters that follow. By itself, it may seem rather abstract, and some readers may wish to read this chapter quickly and then return to it after reading the six that follow.

To get at the Hindu idea of creation, we will study a creation myth from the *Brhadaranyaka Upanishad,* which throughout I will translate simply as *The Great Forest Teaching.* Though this myth is well over twenty-five hundred years old and not widely known today, it indicates features of Indian thinking about beginnings, creation, and creativity that are basic and influential even today. Let us first read the whole myth and then explore it section by section.

In the beginning, this universe was self, in the form of Person. The Person looked around and saw nothing other than himself. First the Person said, "I am," and thus the word "I" originated. Therefore, even now, when addressed a person first responds, "I am," and afterward says whatever other name he has.[1]

The Person was afraid, and therefore whoever is all alone is afraid. But the Person reflected, "Since there is nothing other than me, of what am I afraid?" Then his fear vanished, for of what could he have been afraid? One becomes afraid only of someone else. But neither did he rejoice, for one who is all alone does not rejoice. The Person desired a second.

Now the Person was of the same size and kind as a man and woman closely embracing. He caused himself to fall into two parts, and from him a husband and wife were born. Therefore the sage Yajnavalkya said, "By oneself, one is like a half-fragment"; but this space is filled by woman. He united with her, and thus humankind was born. But the woman reflected, "How can he unite with me after engendering me from himself? For shame! I will conceal myself."

She became a cow; he became a bull and united with her, and from this all cattle were born. She became a mare; he became a stallion. She became a female ass; he became a male ass and united with her, and from this all whole-hooved animals were born. She became a she-goat; he became a billy-goat. She became a ewe; he became a ram and united with her, and from this all goats and sheep were born. Thus he created all pairs, down even to the ants.

The Person realized, "I, indeed, am this creation, for I emitted it all from myself." Thus creation arose. Whoever knows this is born in that creation of his. Then he rubbed his hands together. From his mouth as the fire-hole and from his two hands rubbed together, he created fire. That is why both mouth and hands are without hair on the inside, for the fire-hole is without hair on the inside.

When a person says "Sacrifice to this god!" "Sacrifice to that god!" speaking of one single god and then another single god, all of this is his own creation, for he is all the gods. Now, whatever is moist he created from semen, and semen is soma, the drink of the gods. All this universe is food and the eater of food. Soma is food, and Fire is the eater of food. This was the surpassing creation of Brahma, for he created the gods, who then were above him. Though mortal, he created the immortals,

---

1. I omit a brief section which explains the etymology of the word "person" in Sanskrit.

and therefore this is a surpassing creation. Whoever knows this is born in that surpassing creation of his.[2]

Let us now consider it section by section.

IN THE BEGINNING, THERE IS ONLY SELF

The myth begins by asserting that before anything else there is always an original self (in this case, described as male), which must notice itself before anything else can happen:

> In the beginning, this universe was self, in the form of Person. The Person looked around and saw nothing other than himself. First the Person said, "I am," and thus the word "I" originated. Therefore, even now, when addressed a person first responds, "I am," and afterward says whatever other name he has.

In the beginning, everything that is and will be is present only within the self; otherwise, there is nothing at all. The self is the source of everything and must find in its own "I" the roots of the complex world it encounters. Without an inward-looking knowledge that first uncovers the self, nothing else can be known. This is true for both world and self, since even the world itself is generated from within the "I" as this "I" realizes and expresses itself.

It seems quite different to say that in the beginning there was only God, and that God created our selves out of nothing at all. The biblical account of God's spirit moving over the original chaos and forming a world from it, in Genesis, highlights creation as the sovereign act of God:

> In the beginning when God created the heavens and the earth, the earth was a formless void and darkness covered the face of the deep, while a wind from God swept over the face of the waters. Then God said, "Let there be light," and there was light. (Gen. 1:1–3)

---

2. This myth is found in the *Brhadaranyaka Upanishad* (*The Great Forest Teaching*), at 1.4.1– 6. I have used the translation found in *Hindu Myths,* ed. and trans. Wendy D. O'Flaherty (New York: Penguin Books, 1984), 34–35. Here and throughout I have drawn on excellent and widely available translations of the texts I cite. For the sake of consistency in this book and to minimize the number of footnotes, however, I have occasionally made small alterations in the translations, as noted with each text. These are invariably minor changes, but I urge the reader also to consult the published translations which I cite.

In India, by contrast, the beginning always follows on something that has gone before. One must look within, not to one who stands beyond us, in order to find the meaning of life.

Because they have no clear-cut starting point, the possibilities latent within the human self are endless. If we want to be creative and learn creatively as we reflect on Hindu wisdom, the same point applies: no encounter with the "other," even with a religion very different from my own, can be fruitful unless I also explore my own self, figuring out who I truly already am, from the beginning. When I encounter religious traditions different from my own, I am not taking up an entirely new topic; I am still exploring myself too. When I know another religion, I know myself anew, differently, more deeply.

STEPPING FORTH — IN FEAR, LONELINESS, LOVE

Once the original self becomes aware of its identity, it is perplexed by its own solitude and begins to battle mixed feelings. It fears being alone, but also fears what is different from itself:

> The Person was afraid, and therefore whoever is all alone is afraid. But the Person reflected, "Since there is nothing other than me, of what am I afraid?" Then his fear vanished, for of what could he have been afraid? One becomes afraid only of someone else. But neither did he rejoice, for one who is all alone does not rejoice. The Person desired a second.

Fear and loneliness compel the self to comprehend itself from new angles, and then to look outside, to see if there is something more than itself. To create is rooted not in self-satisfaction but in need; it is only in confrontation with the possibilities of fear and loneliness that the self moves outward beyond its given, ordinary self: the original person desired a second.

If we say that we want to explore Hindu wisdom, for instance, then we need to ask ourselves where this desire comes from. Sometimes we look beyond our own familiar religious selves because we find them lacking, because we need something more than we already are and possess. Or perhaps we are afraid when we look around and notice strange religions which do not fit our expectations, which seem to be growing, which crowd in upon us. We realize that we cannot run the other way; we need to learn about these religions, to comprehend them and respond to them creatively. Perhaps, too, we reach out because we want to live more fully, becoming more than we are already. We may want to end our isolation from those around us, to communicate with them, to give and receive in a living and spiritual way. This is a kind of love which pushes us gently — or fiercely — beyond our settled boundaries, to have hearts as large as the world. Under such conditions — need or fear or love — I meet what is new in terms of what is already happening inside me. As I already am, I encounter a Hindu wisdom that seems new to me.

The myth tells us that when the self faces the challenge of the other and is no longer able to retreat into self-contentment, this is a sign of the spiritual maturity which is at the root of creativity. Mahasweta Devi, whom we shall meet in chapter 7, suggests that the goal of being human is to stop being a spectator, anywhere in life — to become irreversibly involved with those whom we used to consider alien to ourselves. Rediscovering ourselves personally and religiously we overcome our isolation and make ourselves honest and true in relation to the new friends and strangers around us.

MORE THAN MYSELF

In the third part of the myth, the original self is stimulated to create, not by fear — for there is no completely alien "other" that could intrude on the self — but from loneliness. But here too it discovers what is already within itself, for it turns out that the original self was not simple and unitary; it already existed in relationship. In the myth, the self realizes itself as male and female:

> Now the Person was of the same size and kind as a man and woman embracing closely. He caused himself to fall into two parts, and from him a husband and wife were born. Therefore the sage Yajnavalkya said, "By oneself, one is like a half-fragment," but this space is filled by woman. He united with her, and thus humankind was born.

To create is to yield to the fact of my own complexity, that I am not a simple being, that I cannot make my life utterly simple and predictable. The need to create comes from within oneself; this need is as strong as the need of male for female, female for male. Once the self becomes male and female, of course, this change cannot be easily undone; it cannot return to simple self-contentment, to comfortable privacy. The original pure solitude turns out to be only the briefest opening moment in a drama of self-discovery. After the first moment, the self is always interacting with its complementary and contrasting other, its male or female, if it is to become itself again.

Genesis too traces the identities of male and female back to the beginning, though the relationship with God differs in the following two passages:

> Then God said, "Let us make humankind in our image, according to our likeness. . . ." So God created humankind in his image, in the image of God he created them; male and female he created them. (Gen. 1:26–27)

And,

> The man gave names to all cattle, and to the birds of the air, and to every animal of the field; but for the man there was not found a helper as his partner. So the Lord God caused a deep sleep to fall upon the man, and he slept; then he took one of his ribs and closed up its place with flesh. And the rib that the Lord God had taken from the man he made into a woman and brought her to the man. Then the man said, "This at last is bone of my bones and flesh of my flesh; this one shall be called Woman, for out of Man this one was taken." Therefore a man leaves his father and mother and clings to his wife, and they become one flesh. And the man and his wife were both naked, and were not ashamed. (Gen. 2:20–25)

Here too, the sources of human identity and human society can be traced back to the first moments of creation. To be human is to be male and female, though it is less clear how this is also the truth of God's identity.

Another ancient Indian myth (perhaps more than three thousand years old) found in the *Shatapatha Brahmana,* i.e., *The Wisdom of a Hundred Paths,* expresses the original differentiation of self still more elementally. In this text it is an ongoing interchange between fire, which eats, and food, which is eaten:

> In the beginning, the Lord of creatures existed alone. He reflected, "How can I produce offspring?" He exhausted himself practicing asceticism, and generated Fire from his mouth. Since he generated Fire from his mouth, Fire is therefore an eater of food. He who knows that Fire is an eater of food becomes an eater of food himself. . . . [3]

Fire turns food into energy by destroying it; without that food, fire itself is destroyed, for it cannot sustain itself by itself. "Food" and the "eating of

---

3. This myth is found in the *Shatapatha Brahmana* (*Wisdom of a Hundred Paths*) at 2.2.4.1–8a. I have used O'Flaherty's translation, *Hindu Myths,* 32–33, with slight adaptations.

food" mark the interconnectedness of creation, the process of making, consuming, re-creating. It is a never-ending transaction in which no boundary is ever completely fixed. The original differentiation starts a process that cannot be stopped; there must be a continuing and changing relationship, as between fire and food, if the self is to keep living.

When we begin to learn from another religious tradition in a creative and spiritual way, we enter into a living relationship with that other tradition. What we first recognize as strange or opposite to us becomes a part of that greater self we are only beginning to understand. We are nourished by that wisdom; it becomes part of who we are. Nothing is really alien to us, even at the start, and the more we learn, the more our spiritual lives are intertwined with the wisdom we encounter.

Religious traditions stand in complementary relationships to one another, they do not flourish if kept rigidly apart; perhaps we need one another to remain alive. If at first we are hesitant in the face of so many religions, it may help to remember that learning religiously is a lifelong process of interchange, acquiring the other, losing oneself, putting oneself back together again. We consume reality, and the other seems to disappear inside us; but we become what we eat, and thus we remain alive, beyond ourselves. We might even imagine religious traditions to be male and female in relation to one another — provided we allow these male and female roles to shift and grow as we give and receive, as we nurture and explore each other's wisdom.

CONFLICT AND COMPLEMENTARITY

The male and the female, the eater and the eaten: these images imply not only a peaceful, mutual satisfaction, but also a program of trial and error, multiple ventures by which the self remakes itself as more than itself, finding nourishment in the other, surrendering to that other. In the next section of *The Great Forest Teaching* myth, the original male-female complementarity quickly descends into pursuit, flight, and conflict. The female reconsiders her relation to the original and seemingly male self and decides to protect herself from the male who rushes upon her:

> But the woman reflected, "How can he unite with me after engendering me from himself? For shame! I will conceal myself."

He needs her, for in having intercourse with her he seeks to overcome his loneliness and to recover the unity he has already lost. But she resists his effort to reverse the process of creation and return so easily to a comfortable past. She keeps resisting and evading his desire, but he keeps pursuing her, violating her again and again in every diverse form:

> She became a cow; he became a bull and united with her, and from this all cattle were born. She became a mare; he became a stallion. She became a female ass; he became a male ass and united with her, and from this all whole-hooved animals were born. She became a she-goat; he became a billy-goat. She became a ewe; he became a ram and united with her, and from this all goats and sheep were born. Thus he created all pairs, down even to the ants.

The self keeps becoming one again, and each time comes apart once more. Each time he seeks to assert complete union, she eludes him, and so the original unity keeps evolving, the world becomes more and more diverse. In Genesis too, humankind and the diversity of the world go together, but the divinely ordained relationship is again very different:

> God blessed them, and God said to them, "Be fruitful and multiply, and fill the earth and subdue it; and have dominion over the fish of the sea and over the birds of the air and over every living thing that moves upon the earth." (Gen. 1:28)

This account is more peaceful than the Hindu account of search and conquest, though it establishes its own pattern of hierarchy and rule. But we also know that in chapter 2 of Genesis the male and female human beings enter a more contentious relationship, as the woman takes the fruit from the tree of the knowledge of good and evil and offers it to her husband. The rules are set by God and are almost immediately violated. In *The Great Forest Teaching,* it is the original rule that creativity is expressed only in the activity of a self which is one, yet always becoming different from itself. In both cases, however, it seems predictable that rules are broken and then mended.

To preserve an original and living unity in reality is not a smooth process, Hindu wisdom advises us; it is a frightening task, dangerous, marked by gain and loss, and we are deeply a part of the world as it changes, grows and fails, as it is born again. Because we try to create, we are alive; because we fail, we keep on living; because we are embodied, we are male and female, we are two seeking to be one again.

In the *Wisdom of a Hundred Paths,* the desire to have and consume the other makes it uncertain that the self can survive at all:

The Lord of creatures reflected, "I have created from myself an eater of food, Fire, but there is no food here other than me, whom he will not eat." Now the earth was bare at that time; there were no plants nor any trees. The Lord of creatures realized this. But Fire turned toward him with an open mouth, and the greatness went out of the terrified Lord of creatures; and his greatness became speech.... He rubbed his hands, and he obtained an offering of clarified butter, an offering of milk. This offering pleased him.... Then the sun rose up and grew hot, and the wind became mighty and blew. Fire turned away, and the Lord of creatures performed the offering. He produced offspring, and saved himself from Fire who was Death and about to devour him. Whoever knows this and offers the Agnihotra, the Fire Offering, produces offspring, just as the Lord of creation produced offspring.

The world must be created over and over, because the original creative impulse is like fire, consuming whatever it touches, making everything a part of itself. To live, to eat, to speak, to have intercourse: these are creative acts in which the self steps outside itself, overcomes what is outside, and draws it within. Differences are consumed, I become myself in a new way, and a new world emerges from inside me.

Learning is like this. Respecting and welcoming Hindu wisdom is ideally an irenic and complementary process; in the end, we may very well affirm more deeply who we are within our own tradition, while realizing that Hindus are in some ways different from us, in some ways like us. So it should be. Yet these myths warn us that this process of interaction is an uneven one, even a dangerous enterprise. To encounter the wisdom of another tradition can also mean misuse, confrontation, and resistance. It can mean taking things out of context, using them for our own purposes and not in the way they were originally intended; we may force ourselves upon another religious tradition, borrowing what it does not wish to lend. We may conjure up, label, and consume "Hindu wisdom" in order to satisfy our own appetites for spiritual nourishment, strengthening our identities by using up another religious tradition. Or the opposite may be true. We may seek out Hindu wisdom with the great hope that it will nourish us and deepen our faith — but find instead that it overwhelms us, drawing us into a way of seeing the world that seems to undermine what we have always believed. We may find our identities consumed, transformed too abruptly by a religious wisdom we had hoped merely to sample. The values are real, and so are the dangers. But this interchange is life itself, it is our world today; being alive religiously places us in a world of gains and losses. We must proceed with a realistic awareness of what we are about, with a respect for how powerful it is to learn the wisdom of another religious tradition.

A WAY OF LIVING, DAY BY DAY

As the metaphors of intercourse and eating suggest, the creative act has to be repeated. Males keep desiring females, mothers must bring new generations to birth, fires must be fed, we become complex and simple, over and over. In the Hindu tradition, this necessary repetition is emphasized through the importance accorded to ongoing ritual performance. *The Great Forest Teaching* indicates a parallel between the creation and the ritual act of lighting a fire:

> The Person realized, "I, indeed, am this creation, for I emitted it all from myself." Thus creation arose. Whoever knows this is born in that creation of his. Then he rubbed his hands together. From his mouth as the fire-hole and from his two hands rubbed together, he created fire. That is why both mouth and hands are without hair on the inside, for the fire-hole is without hair on the inside.
>
> When a person says "Sacrifice to this god!" "Sacrifice to that god!" speaking of one single god and then another single god, all of this is his own creation, for he is all the gods. Now, whatever is moist he created from semen, and semen is soma, the drink of the gods. All this universe is food and the eater of food. Soma is food, and Fire is the eater of food.

To generate fire out of oneself, and to offer liquids into fire — milk or butter or the intoxicating herb known as soma — suggests that the roots of ritual lie within ourselves; by the rites we perform, we recover the original creative act in a controlled and predictable fashion. When ritual predominates, creativity is formalized and loses some of its spontaneity, but ritual also makes it possible to share the creative act more widely, even with those who have forgotten how to be creative.

This transformation of creativity in ritual is suggested by *The Wisdom of a Hundred Paths,* in a passage we have already seen:

> He rubbed his hands, and he obtained an offering of clarified butter, an offering of milk. This offering pleased him.... Whoever knows this and offers the Agnihotra, the Fire Offering, produces offspring, just as the Lord of creatures produced offspring.

Fire marks the heat of creativity within us, the deep longing of the self, the desire for sexual encounter; and it is also the ritual fire lit in the darkness of the early morning. This morning ritual is the most common of orthodox Hindu rites, the Agnihotra, or Fire Offering. Traditionally it was obligatory upon higher-caste Hindu men, although as we look back from our current vantage point, it is also clear that the symbolism of the ritual was never exclusively "male." In performing this Fire Offering at sunrise and sunset by pouring milk into a fire while saying certain prayers, ritual practitioners marked the natural transition between night and day and remembered the original emergence of self and world from darkness. Thus they created for themselves a conscious harmony with world and self, every day.

In later Hindu traditions, this regular Fire Offering is interiorized in various ways. Various internalized rites seem to have been developed largely for pragmatic reasons, for those unable to light the ritual fires — e.g., for travelers, the ill, the aged — though such rites also took on great symbolic meaning. Sometimes the simple act of eating food becomes a ritual offering into the internal digestive fire, while at other times a strictly mental offering is made. Such rites are striking because they make the human body, its functions, and its internal life force into the new physical and spiritual location for religious practice.

When a person performs these external or internal daily rites with full consciousness of what the offering means, the act illuminates in a small, sacramental fashion the cycle of creativity, the gains and losses that come when the self steps beyond its original boundaries. The energies and dangers of creation are woven into everyday life, daily gains and losses sacramentalized as a regular way of life where we keep creating ourselves.

So too for us: if we are to learn from India, we must look into Hindu wisdom not just once or in moments of spontaneous enthusiasm, but with awareness and forethought, in regular ways and over long periods of time. The creativity of the search needs to infuse our lives over the long run, as the balance of self-awareness and openness becomes integral to who we are as persons. To learn from India needs to become as regular a habit as eating, as regular as the changing of night into day. When we seem to have no creative energies and seem to be learning nothing, it is this habitual commitment that will keep us on the path of learning wisdom and making it our own. The six chapters that follow are meant simply to offer six ways to begin making such learning something we can share regularly, religiously, ritually, at least as a part of our lives.

TO CREATE IS TO DIE

The Hindu myths of creation also remind us that if we are serious about making the creative act central to our lives, we have to encounter and even embrace the reality of death. Like the chill darkness that follows sunset, the burning low of a fire, the exhaustion of food, the weariness of lovers, creativity wanes; persons who extend themselves to make new worlds in the end still have to face the return of fears about who they are, that original loneliness. The *Wisdom of a Hundred Paths* puts it this way:

> Fire turned away, and the Lord of creatures performed the offering. He produced offspring, and saved himself from Fire who was Death and about to devour him. Whoever knows this and offers the Agnihotra, the Fire Offering, produces offspring, just as the Lord of creatures produced offspring. In this way he saves himself from Fire, from death, when he is about to devour him. Whenever one dies and is placed in the fire, he is reborn from the fire just as he is born from his mother and father, for fire consumes only his body.

Fires continue to burn only if they continue to consume, never standing still. To create, we must resist the temptation to stop extending ourselves in new possibilities. To live wisely, we must keep letting go of ourselves, and this is not a smooth or easy process.

If we learn well from India, we have to keep letting go of what we already are; the process will not end where we happen to be at any given time. When we have learned enough, we will have stopped becoming wise; when we are fully satisfied, we are dead. If we let another religion touch us deeply enough so that we truly learn from it, we have to keep letting go of what we have already been, who we think we already are. Opening our hearts, making them as wide as the world, thinking across religious boundaries: these are acts of the living, but they also mean dying just a bit every day.

J. Krishnamurti, a renowned spiritual teacher who died in 1986, gained wide respect because of his skill in helping people to think and live beyond their accustomed and narrow ways of imagining themselves and their spiritual possibilities. He put the basic issue this way, very simply:

> Dying is part of living. You cannot love without dying, dying to everything which is not love, dying to all ideals which are the projection of your own demands, dying to all the past, to the experience, so that

you know what love means and therefore what living means. So living, loving, and dying are the same thing, which consists of living wholly, completely, now. Then there is action which is not contradictory, bringing with it pain and sorrow; there is living, loving and dying in which there is action. That action is order. And if one lives that way — and one must, not in the occasional moments but every day, even every minute — then we shall have social order. . . . So to live is to love and to die.[4]

Of course, if we do not really want to learn, if our interest in Hindu wisdom is only a mild curiosity, if we intend not to change, then it may be better not to start at all. As the following chapters will show, learning from India entails looking at ourselves in a thoroughly realistic and unromantic way, looking for a God who is terrible to behold, letting go of our settled images of what God is like, allowing God — or the Goddess — to be found in absolutely every human experience, even in the most horrific and banal violence of modern times. We may find it difficult to undertake this learning, and harder still to keep rethinking ourselves in the process. But the choice itself is a creative and spiritual opportunity.

SELF SURPASSES SELF

Fortunately, the ongoing encounter with death need not be where things end. Though deeply intertwined with self and governed by its inner possibilities and limits, the act of creation goes beyond this self, even beyond death. As *The Great Forest Teaching* puts it, to create is to create the gods themselves:

> When a person says "Sacrifice to this god!" "Sacrifice to that god!" speaking of one single god and then another single god, all of this is his own creation, for he is all the gods. . . . This was the surpassing creation of Brahma, for he created the gods, who then were above him. Though mortal, he created the immortals, and therefore this is a surpassing creation. Whoever knows this is born in that surpassing creation of his.

It may seem odd to say that we create our religious world, even the gods themselves. As we shall see, most Hindus, today as in the past, assert the

---

4. *Flight of the Eagle* (New York: Harper and Row, 1971), 77.

existence of a God or Goddess beyond anything that humans can make up; Hindus do not think of themselves as creating Krishna or Shiva or Kali, the great deities whom we shall consider in chapters 4, 5, and 6. But for now the point is simply that in every true act of creation self exceeds self; it discovers and forms what is beyond itself, more than it could hope or expect by any practical calculation. When the self has faced death and then recovers itself in religious realities beyond what it can assimilate or entirely control, it is more than it could ever have been before. In its search, the self forms and names the religious realities by which it expresses its hopes and desires, it gives names and forms to what is greater than itself: it creates the gods. This is religious ecstasy, where creativity is fulfilled, where human realities open into divine possibilities. Our daily efforts to learn result in a wisdom beyond what we can even imagine.

Here too we could profitably explore how understandings of creation, self, and God are woven together in religious traditions where it would be even more surprising to assert that humans in some way shape the divine. Such comparisons and contrasts help us to see what is distinctive to Hindu wisdom, to appreciate its traditions in new ways. For instance, the early Jewish tradition offers powerful insights into how self-identity is formed in the presence of God the creator:

> To whom then will you compare me,
> or who is my equal? says the Holy One.
> Lift up your eyes on high and see:
> Who created these?
> He who brings out their host and numbers them,
> calling them all by name;
> because he is great in strength,
> mighty in power,
> not one is missing.
> Why do you say, O Jacob,
> and speak, O Israel,
> "My way is hidden from the Lord,
> and my right is disregarded by my God"?
> Have you not known? Have you not heard?
> The Lord is the everlasting God,
> the Creator of the ends of the earth.
> He does not faint or grow weary;
> his understanding is unsearchable.
> He gives power to the faint,

and strengthens the powerless.
Even youths will faint and be weary,
and the young will fall exhausted;
but those who wait for the Lord
shall renew their strength,
they shall mount up with wings like eagles,
they shall run and not be weary,
they shall walk and not be faint.

(Isa. 40:25–31)[5]

This is a wisdom that traces creation back to God, the beginning of all things; to find oneself is to find oneself in God alone. As we read *The Great Forest Teaching,* it is well to keep in mind Isaiah's vision of God the Creator and human beings in need of God. If we have grown up in a biblical tradition, it is all the more wise for us to reflect on the mystery of original self and the ecstasy by which all spiritual things arise from within.

BEGINNING TO LEARN FROM HINDU WISDOM

The endeavor to learn from India leads us beyond the boundaries of our own tradition, how we have already known and named and encountered God. We gain more from this wisdom than we give in the search; we become more than we could have been before. In the end, we may find ourselves thinking and imagining God in terms we had not known previously, terms neither entirely our own nor entirely borrowed from somewhere else. We have consumed both the old and the new, and they have become part of us. We do what we can, we reach our limits, and God meets us just beyond our limits. If we are blessed, Hindu wisdom speaks God to us.

If there is some truth in the points made in the preceding pages, then there is much in Hindu wisdom for us to observe, enjoy, and take to heart; the possibilities that open before us will be almost infinite. The particularities of Hindu wisdom which we will observe in the next chapters — quite aside from the question of how well I manage to present them! — can affect us powerfully. But it should be clear that there is no room for mere spectators. We must explore with open minds, mindful that even as we begin to read, we are already more involved than we quite understand. We must be careful and prudent as we learn, for we are not the lords of creation; our world —

---

5. All biblical translations are from the New Revised Standard Version, as found in the New Oxford Annotated Bible (New York: Oxford University Press, 1991).

perhaps especially our religious world — arises from within us, but it is older than we are and it will outlast us.

I mentioned at the start of this chapter that it is rather abstract, primarily a guide to what follows. Whether it has any practical value will be measured as we explore examples of Hindu wisdom in the next six chapters. Let us see what it means to realize that there is only one true self (chapter 2); how the Buddha found in his own life story the seeds of lasting freedom (chapter 3); how whole religions can be built around seeing and not-quite-seeing Krishna (chapter 4); how the deeds of Shiva draw us into a world of sacred scandal and divine mystery (chapter 5); how the Goddess, Mother of the universe, pervades the entire world and the self (chapter 6); how in our own time Mohandas Gandhi and Mahasweta Devi have explored and ventured to put in writing the interconnections among self, truth, nonviolence, and God (chapter 7). As we undertake these experiments, we shall try, as best we can, to learn from Hindu wisdom, in the process re-creating our religious selves.

2

Nothing but Self

If we want to become wise by learning from India, one of the first lessons India teaches us is that we must expand our sense of self. Even in ancient times, some Hindus went so far as to understand the self as the greatest, simplest, and most complete of all realities. What I know about myself in daily life only hints at a much deeper, more everlasting inner self: self, my mere and ordinary self, gives an inkling of the original and supreme self which is the source of everything else.

Almost three thousand years old, the following story tells about how a man named Uddalaka explained the nature of reality to his son Svetaketu. When Svetaketu reaches the proper age, Uddalaka sends him to study the Vedas, the ancient body of hymns composed in praise of the ancient pantheon of gods and used in ritual:

> There was one Svetaketu, of the family of Aruni. One day his father said to him: "Svetaketu, take up the celibate life of a student, for there is no one in our family, my son, who has not studied, who is the kind of Brahmin who is a Brahmin only because of being born one." So he went away to become a student at the age of twelve and learned all the Vedas.

By the time Svetaketu returns, though, he has learned mainly to think highly of himself:

> He returned when he was twenty-four, swell-headed, thinking himself to be learned; he was arrogant. His father then said to him, "Svetaketu, here you are, my son — swell-headed, thinking yourself to be learned, and arrogant. Didn't you ask about that rule by which one hears what

has not been heard of before, thinks of what has not been thought of before, and perceives what has not been perceived before?" (*Chandogya Upanishad* 6.1.1–3)[1]

Svetaketu admits that he has not learned this rule, how to move from the things we see to their underlying source, for no one taught him about that. Uddalaka then undertakes to teach him how the world arises from self, according to this creation myth:

> In the beginning, son, this world was simply what is existent — one only, without a second.... And the existent thought to itself: "Let me become many. Let me propagate myself." It emitted heat. The heat thought to itself: "Let me become many. Let me propagate myself." It emitted water.... The water thought to itself: "Let me become many. Let me propagate myself." It emitted food.... (*Chandogya Upanishad* 6.2.1, 3, 4)

As Uddalaka continues teaching, he focuses increasingly on the mystery of self which underlies the creative process and even the whole world. By a series of simple analogies and evocative images he helps Svetaketu to understand the truth of a simpler, higher self, the deeper mystery that underlies all reality. Just as a true and everlasting self lies within my ordinary, everyday self, so too the manifold realities and differences within the world point beyond themselves to an underlying universal reality, called Brahman. The convergence of the true self and the world's inner self is indicated by the Sanskrit-language phrase *tat tvam asi* — you are that, i.e., you are that highest reality, Brahman.

In teaching his son, Uddalaka repeats, "You are that!" eight times, each time with a different illustration. First, just as the essences of different flowers become honey so pure that one cannot trace the honey back to any particular flower, so everything reaches the fullness of Being and thereafter cannot be traced back to any individual source. Second, just as rivers arise due to rain from the ocean and then flow back into it and ultimately do not keep an identity separate from it, so all beings come from and return to the highest reality. Third, just as sap flows everywhere through a tree and gives it life, so the self flows everywhere throughout all reality. Fourth, the fig seed is the smallest of all seeds, but from it comes a great tree; so too, although we cannot see the essence from which all else comes, it is surely there. Fifth,

---

1. Translations from the *Chandogya Upanishad,* here and below, are from the translation by Patrick Olivelle in the *Upanisads* (Oxford: Oxford University Press, 1996), with slight adaptations.

just as salt dissolved in water can be tasted everywhere but is seen nowhere, so too true Being pervades reality without being seen in any particular place. Sixth, just as a man who is blindfolded and abandoned in a strange place will need help in finding his way even to his own home, so too we need guidance to recover our own deepest selves. Seventh, just as a dying man retreats into himself, loses worldly consciousness, and lets go of all that is not really his self, so too we must let go of everything that is not self. Eighth, just as an honest man who is on trial will not be burnt if he touches the red-hot axe, so the truth will become clear if it is truly tested.

These eight analogies offer ways to begin understanding the underlying, fundamental unity of reality, but the teaching as a whole is intended to change the way Svetaketu thinks, helping him gradually to achieve lasting self-knowledge. The self — the true self which must be traced deeper, from my everyday self — is the deepest, most subtle, most original, most important thing that can be known; it is all-important that one not give up before reaching that knowledge. The way is surely difficult, and the ancient texts always emphasized how difficult the path to self-knowledge is, how few people ever attain it. But we can gradually find our way to that knowledge if we search for self and in the process reconsider everything else, over and over. As we have already seen in chapter 1, true creativity and true freedom, which mark the ability to step fruitfully beyond ourselves, inevitably mean that we will come face to face with our deepest selves. If we want to be happy, we need to know and be at peace with who we are. If we want to create, we have to search those selves, let go of them and move beyond them, searching until we can go no farther. Many classic texts testify to this interest in the self, but the *Chandogya Upanishad* is probably the most influential.

Indian thinkers, ancient and modern, have believed in the reality and value of this deeper inner self, but most have maintained some sense of difference, as if to say: "Yes, the true self of all reality lies within my self, and from my everyday self I can trace a path to the self of all. I encounter that ultimate self; I live within its all-encompassing reality. But I am not the ultimate self." This moderate stance is accepted even in most of the schools of Vedanta, which dedicated themselves to understanding and applying the wisdom of the Upanishads. But one Vedanta school, the Advaita, or nondualist, school, pushed matters to the limit, saying that if we truly understand what it means to speak of self, we will realize that this self cannot be confined at all. When the nonessentials have been stripped away, we will see that there is only one true self for all reality. The nondualists meant very seriously that self and highest reality mirror one another: to know my self fully is to know everything, because the self, my true self, actually *is* everything. According to nondualist Vedanta there is no enduring difference between the individual self and the self of the universe, i.e., Brahman. There is no duality; there is nothing which is not my self.

The nondualists knew very well that it is not useful merely to make great claims about self; to equate my everyday self with the self of all is arrogant, and useless too. Students must be helped to translate this simplest of all truths into a practical wisdom which transforms them and gives them deeper life. Many Vedanta texts seek to inculcate this useful discovery of the true self, both the theory and a way to appropriate it practically; one of the most vivid is the *Vivekacudamani* (i.e., *The Crest Jewel of Discrimination*). This small classic of 580 verses was composed sometime after the year 800. It is a very focused, thoughtful distillation of the Upanishadic teaching on self. It insists on the ultimate unity of self and Brahman and uses the story of a teacher and his student to describe in vivid terms the process by which a person comes to realize this unity, and thus to become completely free. Let us examine the *Crest Jewel* and assess how it challenges us to rethink what we mean by self.[2]

The *Crest Jewel* identifies four stages in this process: first, an initial crisis, a dissatisfaction with my self as I experience it now, and thus a sorely felt need to know some more lasting truth; second, a realization of who I am not; third, a realization, first in theory and then in practice, of who I truly am; fourth, the realization of this self-knowledge in a radically changed way of life. Let us consider these stages one by one.

A NECESSARY IDENTITY CRISIS

The first stage is crisis. At the beginning of the *Crest Jewel* the would-be student is desperate, and he seeks out the teacher.[3] The student is in crisis because the world torments him by its constant change and fluctuation; nothing is permanent, nothing can be relied on. The world is an ocean in which he is drowning, a fire by which he is withered and burnt. His opening words effectively present his torment:

---

2. I have discussed the nature of nondualist (Advaita) Vedanta in more technical detail in my book *Theology after Vedanta: An Experiment in Comparative Theology* (Albany: State University of New York Press, 1993).

3. Both teacher and student in the *Crest Jewel* are male, and I shall refer to them as male. Vedanta is one of many traditional religious systems, East and West, which traditionally assumed that those who study and teach should be male. Today, though, this assumption has been questioned, and there are women who study and teach Vedanta.

O Master, O friend of those that bow to you! You are an ocean of mercy, I bow to you. Lift me, fallen as I am into this sea of becoming, by a straightforward glance of thine eye which sheds nectar-like supreme compassion. Save me from death, afflicted as I am by the unquenchable fire of the blaze of this world of suffering, and shaken violently by the winds of an untoward lot, terrified and so seeking refuge in you, for I do not know any other person with whom to seek shelter. (vv. 35–36)

O Lord, with your nectar-like speech, sweetened by the enjoyment of the elixir-like bliss of Brahman, pure, cooling to a degree, issuing in streams from your lips as from a pitcher, and delightful to the ear — sprinkle me who am tormented by worldly afflictions as by the tongues of a forest-fire. Blessed are those on whom even a passing glance of your eye lights, accepting them as your own. How can I cross this ocean of becoming? What is to be my fate? Which means should I adopt? I know nothing about these matters. Have mercy on me, Lord, and bring to an end the misery of this world of suffering.

Thus the student speaks, and he takes refuge, scorched by the heat of the burning fire of this world of suffering. . . . (vv. 39–41a)[4]

Since he is thoroughly dissatisfied with the world, he is also vulnerable, open and ready to accept any solution, any escape. The teacher seems always to have been available to anyone who would seek his help, but only now can he help this particular student, because he has asked to be taught. All that follows is the teacher's great act of compassion, as he exposes the false self and shows to the student his true but forgotten identity.

LEARNING WHO I AM NOT

The second step, then, is the teacher's project of uncovering the student's false self-understanding; he shows him that he is not who he thought he was. We might imagine that ignorance is simply the problem of not knowing one thing or another. But the *Crest Jewel* says that the problem of ignorance goes very deep; it affects not only our minds, but our whole lives and experience of the world around us. Ignorance is a very basic confusion about who we are and how we are to live; it is a primordial confusion, a mistaken identity and mistaken way of life; in Sanskrit, this is called *maya*, profound confusion.

---

4. Throughout, I use Swami Madhavananda's 1921 translation: *Vivekacudamani of Sri Shankaracarya* (Calcutta: Advaita Ashrama, 1992), with slight adaptations.

This profound confusion permeates our normal way of thinking, acting, and living. It infuses the entire make-up of what we are, and produces the world as we experience it:

> The body, organs, breath, mind, ego, etc., all modifications, the sense-objects, pleasure and the rest, the gross elements such as the ether, in fact, the whole universe, even undifferentiated matter — all of this is non-self. From prime matter down to the body, everything is confusion and the effect of confusion. Know these and confusion itself to be non-self, and therefore unreal, like a mirage in the desert. (vv. 122–23)

The student's dark tendencies and passions draw him downward and distort reality for him. Unaware, he projects a wrong version of the reality, and thus distorts his every experience. He cannot find himself and cannot understand the simple, clear truth that self is everything, so he turns life into a great problem. He finds the world complex and divided, although in reality it is very simple. Even his essential goodness — which leads him intuitively toward the truth — is still mixed with confusion; his misery has prompted him to seek out a teacher, but it also makes it very difficult for him to listen. Though the Hindu tradition does not identify a single starting point for all that is wrong in the world, we must be reminded here of the Christian teaching on original sin. Before and deeper than any wrong that we ourselves do, there is already disorder deep within us; we are pulled in many ways at once, we cannot just save ourselves, we do not even know who we are.

According to the *Crest Jewel,* the remedy for the human plight is first of all the activity indicated in its title: we need to learn *discrimination,* the ability to distinguish one thing from another properly and, ultimately, self from everything that is not self. The *Crest Jewel* is committed to the value of right knowledge, the accurate, discriminating process of discernment which clarifies our reality and makes us free. By subtle, discerning knowledge, humans can sort out the distortions in reality, observe them dispassionately, and become detached from them. The teacher explains:

> It is truly through your connection with ignorance that you, who are the supreme self, find yourself bound to non-self, from which alone proceeds the flow of this world. The fire of knowledge, kindled by discrimination between these two [self and non-self], will burn up the effects of ignorance together with its roots. Now I am going to tell you fully what you ought to know, the discrimination between self and non-self. Listen to it and confirm it in your own self. (vv. 47, 71)

Discrimination is the means to the destruction of confusion:

> Confusion can be destroyed by the realization of pure Brahman, one
> without a second, just as the mistaken idea of a snake is removed by
> the discrimination that the apparent snake is a rope.... This realization
> is achieved by perfect discrimination between self and non-self; there-
> fore one must distinguish between the individual self and the true self.
> (vv. 110, 203)

To distinguish and sort out the real from the unreal is most prominent in the
first part of the *Crest Jewel;* the teacher helps the student to become a self-
controlled person who can see things — sense objects, mental impressions
and developed ideas, dreams and fancies, the words and rules and practices
of religious life — exactly as they are, nothing less or more. This discernment
is analytic; it breaks down the non-self, taking it apart piece by piece: just
take a closer look, and notice that you are not what you seem to be; examine
your body, and guess how long it is likely to last; search out the vital force of
life within you, but see how frail and passing your breath is; reflect upon the
workings of your mind, but see how many limitations constrain your ability
to think clearly; admire your deeper levels of awareness and understanding,
but please admit the fluctuations and gaps in this understanding, how hard it
is to live a fully aware life, how easy it is to slip into fossilized self-images;
admit your deepest inner joy, but admit how fragile and fleeting are your
experiences of that joy.

In each instance — body, life, mind, understanding, joy — the teacher offers a series of analyses and arguments as to why such things cannot be
the true self. They are impermanent, they keep changing, they depend on
other realities, and so they cannot be the true, fundamental self which is always utterly simple and free. To realize all this is the fruit of discrimination;
layers of non-self are peeled away, each revealed to be empty, nothing inside it but another empty formulation of identity. By seeing what the self is
not, ignorance is stripped bare of its disguises, uncovered in all its deceptive
multiplicity. An honest, clear look at ourselves confirms the deep roots and
pervasiveness of confusion and the futility of the claims we habitually make
about being ourselves, improving ourselves, finding ourselves.

The teacher reinforces the uncovering of non-self by getting the student
also to draw back from thoughtless and superficial ways of living. The non-
self must be experienced as repulsive if the student is to turn away from
it in real life; the teacher instills in the student a felt repugnance for the
corruptible body, its flaws and miseries:

This body of ours is the product of food and comprises our material layer. It lives on food and dies without it; it is a mass of skin, flesh, blood, bones, and filth, and can never be the eternally pure, self-existent self. How can this body, being a pack of bones, smeared with flesh, full of filth and highly impure, be the self-existent self, the knower, which is ever distinct from it? It is a foolish person who identifies himself with a mass of skin, flesh, fat, bones, and filth, while the person skilled in reflection knows his own self, the only reality there is, as distinct from the body. (vv. 154, 158–59)

Though body itself is not the real problem — it is just body, after all — it symbolizes all the appearances, transitory realities, and ultimate disappointments on which the confused person pins his or her hopes.

The student strips away every illusion; mind and heart are deprived of their comforting illusions, until nothing at all conceals them. Indeed, at the end of the first half of the *Crest Jewel,* the student is left only with a stark realization that nothing endures, that nothing he knows from ordinary life can be the self. He has advanced in learning, but this throws him into a great perplexity, for he is faced with sheer nothingness. He cries out,

After these five layers — body, breath, mind, understanding, joy — have been eliminated as false then, teacher, I find nothing left but the absence of everything! What is there with which the wise knower of self can realize identity? (v. 212)

The honesty of the situation is startling. The best, clearest, and most open-minded inquiry does not pay off in uplifting affirmations and immediate rewards. It is the good student who is left at the edge of the abyss. He has lost his grip on everything he had; he has not yet gained anything back.

Perhaps it is this way when we start to learn from another religion too. If we really open our minds and hearts, in the short run we may end up disillusioned, as if to share the student's realization: "My faith is not what I believed it to be; my religion is not unique, as I had thought it to be; I am not gaining from this other religion the wisdom and comfort I had expected. What I used to think was solid and true now seems artificial and arbitrary. Being spiritual is not as sure and simple as I had thought it to be; it is not identical with the things I was taught when I was young, nor is it the things I have kept doing because I never took alternatives seriously. So what is really spiritual? What can I really depend on? Everything? Nothing at all? And does it even matter?"

FINDING MY SELF, IN THEORY AND PRACTICE

The student has no follow-up plan, so it is up to his teacher to offer him some new insight which can take him beyond this new desolation, his sense of utter emptiness. The third part of the *Crest Jewel* is dedicated to describing how a person can come to discover self and again become integrated and whole. On one level, the teacher's task is simple; he just has to get the student to look at himself again, this time even more closely. The teacher already knows that there is a single, all-encompassing self, and this true self has already been announced in the Upanishads, particularly in the *Chandogya,* which we examined above. In the beginning, everything was one, there was no dividing of reality into parts. Your own self, he tells the student, is really the self of the universe, one without a second. When you realize this, ordinary consciousness will be decisively transformed, the obsessions of restricted, ordinary consciousness shattered, the constraints which diminish self will be cast off:

> The self is full, without beginning or end, immeasurable, unchanging, it is only one, not two, it is Brahman. Here there is no diversity whatsoever. The self is not to be avoided nor taken up nor accepted nor relied upon; it is only one, nondual, Brahman. Here there is no diversity whatsoever. It is without qualities or parts, subtle, unvarying, without color; it is only one, nondual, Brahman. Here there is no diversity whatsoever. (vv. 464, 467, 468)

To convey this truth, the teacher returns to the *Chandogya Upanishad*'s "You are that — you are that highest reality, Brahman" (*tat tvam asi*). He takes seriously the tension between the everyday "you" and the ultimate "that," between what we seem to be and what we truly are; he emphasizes the creative possibilities provoked by this obvious tension: think back and forth, scrutinize your ordinary self as you know it, but also envision the largest view of reality you can imagine. Believe scripture, which tells you that your self is the self of all, and little by little adjust your way of thinking so that you can glimpse this amazing truth.

Once the teacher has declared the truth of nondualism in general, he also shows the student how to think differently about himself in particular. He appeals to him to change his way of life, to learn by practice to see the deeper and unchanging self that is beyond and beneath our ordinary self. At a key point in this teaching, he repeats ten times a refrain which encourages transformation: "You are that Brahman: establish this attitude in your self!"

> That which is beyond caste and creed, family and lineage; devoid of name and form, quality and flaw; transcending space, time, and sense-objects — *you are that Brahman: establish this attitude in your self!*
>
> That supreme Brahman which is beyond the range of all speech but is accessible to the eye of pure realization; which is pure, the embodiment of knowledge, the beginningless entity — *you are that Brahman: establish this attitude in your self!*
>
> That which is free from birth, growth, development, waste, disease, and death; which is indestructible, the cause of the projection, maintenance, and dissolution of the universe — *you are that Brahman: establish this attitude in your self!*
>
> That beyond which there is nothing, higher than the highest, the inmost self, of unitary essence, the real, conscious, joyful, infinite and immutable — *you are that Brahman: establish this attitude in your self!*
> (vv. 254, 255, 258, 263)

When the *Crest Jewel* combines a new understanding of self with the determination to live according to this understanding, this is best thought of as a kind of intellectual yoga. Persistent practice brings home what one has learned intellectually: integrate yourself clearly, simply, without distraction; learn to be at home with your own true self. What you have found not to be true, by uncovering what you are not and, positively, by hearing the truth of self declared to you — make all that your own truth, bear it within your heart, find your self in that truth:

> This imaginary world has its root in mind and never persists after the mind is annihilated. Therefore integrate mind in the supreme self which is your inmost essence. Through total integration, the wise one realizes in the heart the infinite Brahman, which is of the nature of eternal knowledge and absolute bliss, which has no exemplar, transcends all limitations, is ever free and without activity, and which is like the limitless sky, indivisible, absolute. With mind integrated, behold self in your self, the self of infinite glory, and cut off your bondage scented with the scents of previous births; strive for the fruition of your birth as a male human being. The self is devoid of all limiting adjuncts, existence, it is

consciousness, bliss, one without a second: firmly establish your self in the self, and you shall no more come this way. (vv. 407–8, 411–12)

This is the same point we noticed in chapter 1: there is a practical side to self-knowledge, whether I am extending myself in the act of creating or more fundamentally recovering myself. As a ritual must be repeated again and again before I can begin to be at home with its rhythms, self-knowledge must be lived with greater and greater focus if I am truly to realize — know, accept, become — who I have always been.

Encountering another religious tradition uncovers much that I have mistakenly thought about myself; the encounter with the unfamiliar expands me beyond what I previously thought possible, illuminating and pushing me beyond the limits I had set for my identity. But all of this means much more if I live the truth in mind and heart, in the habits of daily life. To understand another tradition, to learn from Hindu wisdom, we need to practice it — in some deliberate way, with some selected text or image or practice — until we realize what Hinduism is not, what it is, how it matters for us, and who we have become in light of it.

CELEBRATING THE ONE TRUE SELF

The fourth part of the *Crest Jewel* celebrates the student's achievement of true self-awareness. At the end of these exercises in thinking clearly and living an integrated life, all at once he realizes the truth of self. As this truth illumines him completely, he stands up and cries out,

My mind is gone, and all its activity has melted away, because I have realized the identity of self and Brahman. I know neither this nor that, nor what or how much is this infinite bliss! The majesty of the ocean of the supreme Brahman, filled with the overflowing nectar bliss of self, cannot be truly expressed in words, nor conceived by the mind. In just the tiniest fraction of it my mind has melted like a hailstone in the ocean. I am now completely filled with just that very bliss. (vv. 481–82)

His way of being and his way of thinking have been forever changed, made utterly simple; discrimination and transformation together have broken the grip of confusion on his mind, heart, and life. The last part of the *Crest Jewel* is devoted to praising this new, totally free state. Just as the experience of confusion was made to feel entirely loathsome, realized self-knowledge is now made as attractive as possible, so that listeners will yearn for this new way of life as they have come to hate their mistaken ways of being.

The teacher now describes the ideal life of the wise person who continues to live in this world, finding it no longer miserable, but entirely blissful. Nothing matters anymore; the wise person plays at all times, in all places and circumstances:

> The illumined sage whose only pleasure is in the self ever lives at ease, whether going or staying, sitting or lying, in every condition.... Satisfied with undiluted, constant bliss, he is neither grieved nor elated by sense-objects, is neither attached nor averse to them, but always plays with the self and takes pleasure therein.
>
> As a child plays with its toys forgetting hunger and bodily pains, exactly so does the person of realization take pleasure in reality, without ideas of "I" or "mine," and is happy.
>
> People who have realized self take their food by begging, without anxiety or humiliation, they drink from the water of rivers. They live freely and independently, and sleep without fear in cremation grounds or forests; their clothing may be simply the air itself, which needs no washing and drying, or the bark of trees. The earth is their bed; they roam the avenue of Vedanta, while their pastime is in the supreme Brahman. The knower of self wears no outer mark and is unattached to external things, rests on this body without identification; he experiences sense-objects just as they come, as others wish, like a child.... (vv. 528, 536–39)

In chapter 1 we saw that solitary self-presence was possible only at the moment before creation; it was an idealized point of origin for the self who would always have to venture outside into a larger world. Now the *Crest Jewel* retrieves that original moment of pure self-presence as a lived reality:

> The sage lives alone enjoying the sense-objects though he is the very embodiment of desirelessness. He is always satisfied with his own self, and he is established as the self of all. Sometimes a fool, sometimes a sage, sometimes possessed of regal splendor, sometimes behaving like a motionless python, sometimes wearing a benign expression, sometimes honored, sometimes insulted, sometimes unknown. Thus lives the wise one, ever happy in the highest bliss. Though without riches, he is ever content; though helpless, he is very powerful. Though not

enjoying sense-objects, he is eternally satisfied. Though unique, he looks upon all with an eye of equality. Though doing things, he is inactive. Though experiencing the fruits of past action, he is untouched by them. Though possessed of a body, he is not identified with it. Though limited, he is everywhere. (vv. 541–43)

If ignorance is a state of mind which deforms our life in this confused and confusing world, then perfect understanding clears the mind and makes the world entirely new. Once the disciple has realized self, he becomes wise and free; the world becomes a realm of freedom, and he can live anew, fully alive.

What are we really hoping for when we seek out the wisdom of another religious tradition? I have indicated several times that we may hope for too much, too quickly, imagining that other religions might give us immediately, upon demand, what we cannot find in our own tradition. But it is also true that we may hope for too little, as if spiritual transformation is available to the lukewarm, those who bury their talents to keep them safe. The *Crest Jewel* dares us to think big, to follow our questions as far as they go: not because we can outrun who we already are, but because at the farthest limit of our minds we will already find ourselves there, beyond the narrow conceptions we put forward as our identities. If we learn Hindu wisdom and make it integral to our lives, we may find out who we are and find that the whole world suddenly and graciously belongs to us: nothing human will be alien to us anymore.

The *Crest Jewel* ends rather simply and undramatically, as the teacher and student bid each other farewell and go their separate ways:

The disciple prostrates before him out of reverence; and then, with his guru's permission, he goes on his way, freed from bondage. The guru, his mind plunged into the ocean of existence and bliss, roams about purifying the whole world, having banished from his mind all ideas which divide things. (vv. 576–77)

Presumably both teacher and student will be available when other seekers start asking questions.

The *Crest Jewel* is representative of a consistent strand of Hindu religious thought. There are always a few students who desire the most basic wisdom of all, that by which everything is known; there are always a few teachers prepared to communicate this knowledge of self, the truth that transforms our thinking and radically changes our lives. Can we share this knowledge and this transformation if we are not Hindus and not properly guided by such a teacher? No, and yes.

"No, we cannot," for we should not assume that we can conduct this search in our own way, as if any plan for the discovery of self is the same as the path indicated by the *Crest Jewel*. The *Crest Jewel* does not allow for every possible meaning of "self," and not every version of self-knowledge is the real thing. But also, "Yes, we can," since the *Crest Jewel* insists that the true road to freedom is marked simply by a clear and undisturbed observation of ordinary life and experience — our bodies, our society, our world as we find it — and a courageous willingness to put aside everything that is unnecessary. The *Crest Jewel* invites every reader to begin reexamining the world and self, just to see where this search might lead.

ONE SELF, TODAY: RAMANA MAHARSHI

Even today, Hindu teachers are received with enormous respect if it is clear that they have personally realized the true self. A famous example is Ramana Maharshi. Born in south India near the end of the nineteenth century, as a boy Ramana seems to have lived in an ordinary fashion, undistinguished by any special interests or aptitudes. But when he was sixteen years old, he had an unexpected and overwhelming experience that completely changed his life. On an ordinary day, without preparation or special circumstances, he suddenly had an overwhelming sense that he was dying. His body went rigid, he lay on the floor, at first terrified but then, gradually, calm and observant. Although his body had gone rigid and might have been dying or already dead, he noticed that he still was conscious, able to observe what was happening. He was not his body, but rather a witness to its drama:

> The shock of death made me at once introspective. I said to myself mentally, "Now death is come. What does it mean? This body dies." As I said this to myself, symptoms of death followed, yet I remained conscious of the inert bodily condition as well as of the "I" quite apart from it. On stretching the limbs they became rigid, breath had stopped and there was hardly any symptom of life in the body. "Well then," I said to myself, "this body is dead. It will be carried to the burning-ground and reduced to ashes. But with the death of the body, am 'I' dead? This body cannot be the 'I,' for it now lies silent and inert, while I feel the full force of my personality, of the 'I' existing by itself — apart from the body. So 'I' am the Spirit, a thing transcending the body." All this was not a mere intellectual process. It flashed before me

vividly as living truth, a matter of indubitable and direct experience, which has continued from that moment right up to this time.[5]

After realizing that he was not his body or anything that could die, he was infused with an abiding sense of self which overwhelmed him and shattered his ordinary consciousness. After Ramana returned to his ordinary physical state, it no longer mattered to him whether he lived or died. He found that he could not live normally anymore. Soon enough, he wandered away from home, taking nothing with him, going forth with no destination in mind. Eventually he stopped at a temple near Arunachala hill in south India, and settled in a cave beneath it. Totally naked, unfed, without concern for his body, he would have died there, were it not for temple devotees who cared for him and nursed him back to health. Only gradually, over the years, did he learn to be gentle with his body; though it was not his own true self, it had nevertheless been given to him for a time. He stayed on at Arunachala for the rest of his life, living quietly near the temple. Like a magnet, this solitary person began to attract visitors from the neighborhood, from other parts of India, and from around the world. The writer Paul Brunton captures something of what it must have been like to meet Ramana, whom he calls the "Sage":

Pin-drop silence prevails throughout the long hall. The Sage remains perfectly still, motionless, quite undisturbed at our arrival.... If he is aware of my presence, he betrays no hint, gives no sign. His body is supernaturally quiet, as steady as a statue. Not once does he catch my gaze, for his eyes continue to look into remote space, and infinitely remote it seems.... There is something in this man which holds my attention as steel filings are held by a magnet. I cannot turn my gaze away from him. My initial bewilderment, my perplexity at being totally ignored, slowly fade away as this strange fascination begins to grip me more firmly. But it is not till the second hour of the uncommon scene that I become aware of a silent, resistless change which is taking place in my mind. One by one, the questions which I prepared in the train with such meticulous accuracy drop away. For it does not now seem to matter whether they are asked or not, and it does not matter whether I solve the problems which have hitherto troubled me. I know only that a steady river of quietness seems to be flowing near me; that a

---

5. As quoted in *Sri Maharshi: A Short Life-Sketch* (Tiruvannamalai: Sri Ramanasramamam, 1973), 2.

great peace is penetrating the inner reaches of my being, and that my thought-tortured brain is beginning to arrive at some rest.[6]

Ramana developed his own unique way of guiding seekers, but the fact that later on he chose to translate the *Crest Jewel* into the Tamil language suggests that he was comfortable with this text's method. He too believed that to know oneself is both a theoretical and practical matter; it clears away wrong ideas and leads to a new sense of identity, and therefore to a new way of life.

Here too, a sense of alternatives can enhance our appreciation of the path offered us by the *Crest Jewel.* How else might I uncover myself so profoundly that I become as it were a different person? I think of the biblical tradition, where selves are transformed by God. This passage from the Acts of the Apostles reports how Saul of Tarsus became a new person:

> Now as Saul was going along and approaching Damascus, suddenly a light from heaven flashed around him. He fell to the ground and heard a voice saying to him, "Saul, Saul, why do you persecute me?" He asked, "Who are you, Lord?" The reply came, "I am Jesus, whom you are persecuting. But get up and enter the city, and you will be told what you are to do." The men who were traveling with him stood speechless, because they heard the voice but saw no one. Saul got up from the ground, and though his eyes were open, he could see nothing; so they led him by the hand and brought him into Damascus. For three days he was without sight, and neither ate nor drank. (Acts 9:3–9)

Saul, now become Paul, regains his sight. Yet he is never the same again, and so he can write, "It is no longer I who live, but Christ who lives in me" (Gal. 2:20). Like Ramana, he too becomes a guide and teacher to others, offering help to those who have not experienced so sudden a transformation.

WHO IS CAPABLE OF KNOWING THE SELF?

People like Ramana testify to the continuing power of the nondualist conviction that there is only one true self. Of course, such stellar examples can also leave us with the uneasy impression that this wisdom is just for the elite few who are willing to leave everything behind. We may find the idea of self-knowledge attractive, but in the end we may wonder whether there isn't

---

6. As quoted in Paul Brunton, *The Maharshi and His Message* (Tiruvannamalai: Sri Ramanasramamam, 1977), 11–14.

too much of a leap to be made, from teachings about non-self to a stark realization of non-self, from promises about nonduality to a complete realization of unity.

Certainly, the *Crest Jewel* does not think that self-knowledge is an easy accomplishment. Indeed, it seems to have low expectations about how much people are capable of. Though self-knowledge may be universally available, the *Crest Jewel* seems to say that most people are incapable of achieving it, not even interested in trying to pursue it:

> Human birth is rare among those who are born; being male is more rare, and being a brahmin is even more rare. Beyond that is focus on the path of vedic dharma, while knowing is beyond that. Distinguishing between self and non-self, experience of one's self, firmness in being *Brahman,* liberation: all this cannot be attained without good deeds done in billions of births. (v. 2)

Skepticism about human interest and human capability seems to be why the *Crest Jewel* puts such a priority on proper birth, education, caste, and gender. The human person is an unruly and undisciplined bundle of possibilities, and needs to be disciplined. This discipline means also that there must be a teacher who has already traveled the necessary path and who can help the seeker draw upon the wisdom of self-knowledge in a way that fits the seeker's life experience and learning. One cannot find the self all by oneself. Since the *Crest Jewel* took for granted the importance of orthodox education, which was restricted to male brahmins, it was these males alone who were designated likely to become successful knowers.

We need not agree with these specific strictures. Most of us will not want to restrict self-knowledge according to gender or class or even literacy, and we may hope for the fulfillment of that other verse, cited earlier:

> That which is beyond caste and creed, family and lineage; devoid of name and form, quality and flaw; transcending space, time, and sense-objects — *you are that Brahman: establish this attitude in your self!* (v. 254)

But the skepticism of the *Crest Jewel* deserves serious consideration, even as we seek to learn from the wisdom of India. On our own, we may be inclined to praise self-knowledge as a wonderful goal and outline the clear, precise steps which any mature, wise, prudent, and utterly committed person can follow in getting there. If so, perhaps we are expecting too much, too easily, in a world where it is very easy for things to go wrong, where many substitutes mask or delay self-knowledge.

To learn from another religion is as simple as coming to self-knowledge — and therefore it is as difficult too. Trying to understand ourselves through drawing on Hindu wisdom can easily go astray. Success is a spiritual accomplishment, not merely an intellectual acquisition or triumph of sincerity and will power. We must be humbly determined to see our own religion and the religions of India just as they are; we must be very clear about our prior religious commitments, willing to grow patiently, learning from our mistakes, seeking guidance from those who have gone before us. Perhaps our quest to learn from India will end in a kind of nondualism, where the wisdom of traditions old and new come together in one simple reality; the *Crest Jewel* suggests that this must be the conclusion. But for now we must make all of this our own wisdom, gradually integrating it with who we are and how we live, in our own time and place, and probably within our original traditions. It is difficult to know the self, and it is difficult to be truly open and truly wise; but the *Crest Jewel* tells us that this is the only journey which makes life worth living.

3

The Buddha Remembered

Hindu wisdom impresses upon us the importance of deepening our sense of self, and we may respond by dedicating ourselves to a search for the deepest and greatest sense of self one can imagine. Like the student in the *Crest Jewel*, we can profit greatly even along the way while we sort out who we are and who we are not. Yet the *Crest Jewel* also tells us that a grand quest for self can be a monumental distraction if we too quickly disregard who we already are, now. It is no small feat to observe and understand our present self, in its present circumstances, without distraction or complication.

It is at this point that the Buddhist tradition can be of help to us. Although it is famous in part for insisting that we need to let go of self and stop seeking after a self we hope exists above and beyond age, suffering, and death, Buddhist teaching also helps us to gain peace and equanimity with who we already are. If we let go of our obsession with bad self and good self, we can live in joy, more peaceful persons now. For this reason we turn now to a consideration of Gautama the Buddha, who teaches us how to recover a sense of who we are now, and thus to find peace in the present moment. We do so not because "Buddhist wisdom" is a subdivision of "Hindu wisdom" — it is not! — but because we are much better off if we appreciate how Hindu and Buddhist thinking have interacted over the centuries. We will grasp Hindu wisdom more fully if we recognize the important contribution made by the Buddha to every Indian's thinking about life and death, bondage and freedom; we will understand the Buddha better if we study him in a broader Indian context, such as is represented by the preceding and following chapters.

THE NOBLE LIFE

A major reason Buddhism so powerfully illuminates the issue of identity is surely the story of the Buddha, Gautama himself. Since the sixth century

B.C.E. his life has inspired and challenged people to take a long, honest look at their own identities. He is a vivid figure, a mirror in whom we can see ourselves; his life story spells out his message on a human scale we can imagine for ourselves too. Tradition portrays his life as the classic story of going forth, search, and discovery. We are told that he grew up in the security of a comfortable palace, unaware of the difficulties of ordinary life and human existence. On three excursions outside the palace he encountered an old person, a sick person, and a corpse being carried to the cremation ground, and he began to meditate on the frailty and brevity of human life. After that, he found no solace in his comfortable surroundings and became dissatisfied with his sheltered life. Finally he fled the palace, escaping to that place of penance and religious quest, the forest. There he studied with various teachers and submitted himself to terrible penances in hopes of unlocking the secret of true peace and freedom. He met with much failure and frustration and suffered terribly, but on that basis gradually became attentive to deeper and simpler spiritual realities. Obstacles cleared away, he was finally able to let go of his narrow identity and his program of self-perfection. He became free, enlightened. In this way, he opened a sure path for countless millions over centuries to come. As Gautama lived and found lasting peace, so can we, for he too experienced human life, its limits, and death too.

It would be ironic, though, were we to idolize him as the privileged possessor of answers to the problems of human existence, for he made wisdom simpler and more direct and stripped away the unnecessary, everything we would be prone to cling to, including hero worship. He did not want to be taken as an answer to other people's problems, for when that happened he too would become a distraction from what people had to find for themselves in their own life experiences.

To understand how we can best learn from the Buddha I have found it helpful to see how he used his own story. For this purpose, I have looked into just one collection of Buddhist texts, the *Middle Length Sayings* (*Madhyama Nikaya*). This is a very ancient collection of 150 episodes and encounters called suttas, which recount how the Buddha lived, how he interacted with a wide variety of people, what he taught. Some suttas are very brief, others much longer. Some remind us of Platonic dialogues, while others are more like scenes from the Gospels. Among the 150 suttas in the *Middle Length Sayings,* I have found only five in which the Buddha tells his own story in detail. This fact itself is important to note: he uses himself as an example sparingly, when it will be helpful.

The Buddha tells his story when he is in conversation with people already willing to listen to him. In sutta 26, he drops by to visit some of his monks who are reflecting on their search for freedom and their efforts to live according to dharma, i.e., according to the way of right thinking and right living which leads to lasting peace. They ask him about his own quest for the dharma. So he tells them his story, interweaving with it the story of how he met and instructed his first disciples. In sutta 4, he speaks about the renunciant's life in the forest and the preparation that is necessary if one is to live there, unprotected yet without fear. He explains how the real dangers of the forest lie inside, not outside, the person; to illustrate this, he tells his own story. In sutta 100, we find a discussion about the sources of authority ascetics might rely on in justifying their practices. The Buddha points out that while many ascetics depend on oral or written traditions, only a few (such as himself) have seen the right way for themselves and teach it from their own experience. He tells his own life story to illustrate this. In sutta 85, the Buddha meets a prince Bodhi and discusses with him whether pain is really necessary on the way to more lasting pleasure. He explains to the prince that pleasure is reached by faith, health, honesty, energy, and understanding; pain may or may not be of any use along the way and should not be sought after. His own life story and seemingly useless penances show that awareness matters, not pain. Suttas 35 and 36 provide the most extensive example. Here the Buddha tells his own story during a long discussion with Sacchaka, a respected ascetic and scholar. In sutta 35 Sacchaka and the Buddha discuss the nature of self; in sutta 36, while they are discussing the nature of bodily discipline, the Buddha tells his story in order to testify to the value of remembering and simple awareness as key to enduring wisdom. In this chapter I focus on this fifth example in order to see how the Buddha tells his story and what we might learn from his wisdom.

WHAT IS A SELF, SACCHAKA?

In sutta 35 Sacchaka is introduced as a great and vigorous debater, quick and clever and serious about religion, a defender of right thought and right action, and eager to silence those who promote improper views and practices. He seems totally in control of his life, articulate, principled, clever — and somewhat cynical too. He already knows that people do not really measure up to their reputations; they do not practice what they preach. When he hears that Gautama teaches that there is no enduring self, Sacchaka is displeased. He is determined to refute Gautama and, accompanied by a large group of followers, he goes to confront him.

When they meet, the Buddha and Sacchaka exchange questions and answers regarding the nature of self. The issue clearly invites broad theoretical consideration, but the Buddha nudges Sacchaka toward the simpler, more probing issue of his own life experience: not, "What is self?" but, "What is your experience of self?" He gradually insinuates himself into Sacchaka's mind, gently unpinning his firmly fixed opinions and unsettling his certainties. He gets him to think more specifically and vividly about self, non-self, and self-control in his own life, asking Sacchaka to reflect on his body, his feelings, his interaction with the world around him, his way of thinking, and even his self-consciousness. Little by little, Sacchaka retreats. In each case, he has to concede that these things are actually much less under his control than he would care to admit; limitations and distractions seem to intrude at every point in life. In fact Sacchaka cannot point to any level of his self that is secure, immune to change, entirely under his control. His theory of self becomes untenable, his set positions come apart under the pressure of the Buddha's scrutiny. His confidence evaporates, his agenda crumbles, his perfectly crafted self-image as defender of the truth falls apart. He becomes just one human being standing before another who understands him. The Buddha suggests to him that it seems neither useful nor true to imagine a self beyond the changing way of things; better to understand and learn to be free in the midst of life as it actually is.

In the end Sacchaka concedes that "self" cannot be the fully accomplished and definite entity he has portrayed it to be. He concludes by graciously offering to host a meal for the Buddha and his disciples. If he is not quite a convert, he is chastened by the more reflective analysis of experience to which the Buddha has led him.

Though the Buddha has little patience with Sacchaka's sense of self and self-importance, he takes him seriously as a person; he engages him directly in order to get him to think clearly and differently. Indeed, the Buddha believes that attentive conversation and clear thinking are at the heart of the religious quest. Questions are important; ideas matter. There is no value in avoiding the implications of our own thinking, nor in settling for sure answers.

Surely we can benefit from this wisdom. Thinking needs to be taken seriously, even if our attention is focused on spiritual matters. Intellectual positions require careful consideration and scrutiny. But if we enjoy the intellectual life, as does Sacchaka, we may tend to quantify and manipulate religion, slipping into intellectual and then spiritual habits and routines which are contrary to our own best interests. Like Sacchaka, we may devote ourselves to what we have found to be the very best way of all, and then assume that this way will lead everyone, everywhere, to a fulfilled, happy self. The

Buddha suggests that we be less possessive of our intellectual prowess and achievements. We need to be ready to keep thinking and learning, for to be alive is an ongoing process. Sacchaka stumbles not because of what he has thought or done, but because he fails to remain attentive and open. At some point he had become content with settled answers, and it is these that the Buddha got him to reconsider, looking afresh at how he actually experienced himself from day to day.

TELL ME ABOUT YOURSELF, BUDDHA

It is during Sacchaka's second visit, recorded in sutta 36, that the Buddha tells him the story of his own search and enlightenment. Perhaps the first visit was a necessary preliminary for this second and more intimate conversation. This time Sacchaka begins by asking about the nature of true bodily development and how bodily discipline relates to development of mind: how does one control and discipline the body, and is there any role for pleasure? He also wants to know a little more about the Buddha: Do you nap in the afternoon? Are you lazy, or a real ascetic like me?

They discuss the relationship between body and mind and the development of the two. Sacchaka mentions physical asceticism, fasts and feasts, and he notes how terribly some ascetics punish themselves. In response to the Buddha's wry observation that many of these ascetics do not look undernourished, Sacchaka suggests that they recover from fasting by eating abundantly. Gautama then raises the question of what is actually conducive to clearing the mind, freeing it from the attraction of pleasure and the fear of pain. When he observes that pleasure is neither to be sought after nor avoided, Sacchaka asks him whether he has ever experienced pleasure. At this point, the Buddha uses his own experience as an example and begins to tell the story of what happened when he was just a young prince:

Before my enlightenment, Sacchaka, while I was still only an unenlightened seeker after enlightenment, I thought, "Household life is crowded and dusty; life gone forth is wide open. It is not easy, while living in a home, to lead the holy life utterly perfect and pure as a polished shell. Suppose I shave off my hair and beard, put on the yellow robe, and go forth from home life into homelessness?" Later, while still young, a black haired young man endowed with the blessing of youth, in the prime of life, and though my mother and father wished otherwise and wept with tearful faces, I shaved off my hair and beard, put on the yellow robe, and went forth from the home life into homelessness.[1]

He bravely goes forth into the forest, but the quest for a better life is not as easy as he had thought. He is disappointed by the teachers with whom he studies. He spends a great deal of time with them and masters what they teach, and each honors him as his most worthy disciple; but he finds that in the end he is no better off than he was at the beginning. Their teachings do not seem to change anything. This learner, at least, must find his own way, if anything is to be gained.

It is helpful for us to take his realization to heart when we seek wisdom. There is no guarantee that the most renowned teachers, the most admired books, the surest paths will actually lead us to a better spiritual state. Even if they have worked in the past, perhaps they may not work for us now. We must be ready to be disappointed in our search for wisdom; and like Gautama, we need to move beyond our disappointment, to seek anew.

First, Gautama takes another wrong turn. He undertakes terrible ascetic practices. He performs violent breathing meditations and undertakes terrible fasts. As a result, he becomes emaciated, dark in color, and near to death. He tries, as he puts it, to crush mind with mind. But still he gains nothing; he does not attain the inner peace he was seeking. At this point he asks himself whether all this pain is really the prelude to lasting joy. He wonders what he has really achieved:

> Whatever recluses or brahmins in the past have experienced, whatever painful, piercing feelings due to exertion, this is the utmost, there is none beyond this. And whatever recluses and brahmins in the future will experience painful, racking, piercing feelings due to exertion, this is the utmost, there is none beyond this. And whatever recluses and brahmins at present experience painful, racking, piercing feelings due to exertion, this is the utmost, there is none beyond this. But by this racking practice of austerities I have not attained any super-human states, any distinction in knowledge and vision worthy of the noble ones. Could there be another path to enlightenment?[2]

---

1. *Majjhima Nikaya* (*The Middle Length Discourses*) 36.12, 13. All quotations are from the English translation *The Middle Length Discourses of the Buddha*, trans. Bhikku Nanamoli and Bhikku Bodhi (Boston: Wisdom Publications, 1995).

2. *The Middle Length Discourses*, 36.30–31.

His energetic and sincere program of self-improvement has not worked, so he stops and thinks.

THE BUDDHA REMEMBERED

When he reflects, a very simple and extraordinary thing happens to Gautama. He remembers a moment much earlier in his life, when he sat down under a tree and without effort reached the peace he has not been able to find in his present intensive search:

> I recall that when my father the Shakyan was working, while I was sitting in the cool shade of a rose-apple tree, quite secluded from sensual pleasures, secluded from unwholesome states, I entered upon and abided in the first stage of meditation, which is accompanied by applied and sustained thought, with rapture and pleasure born of seclusion.

He reviews his strenuous and fruitless activity in light of that earlier easy and untroubled moment:

> Could that have been the path to enlightenment? Then, following on that memory, came the realization, "That was indeed the path to enlightenment!"[3]

What he was looking for had been given to him for free, much earlier in his life. He searched because he had forgotten that earlier moment; the fruit of his search was not something new, but the ability to remember what had happened once before. Remembering how he had found peace under the rose-apple tree transformed his present moment and even prepared the way for his enlightenment, which would follow shortly.

In a much later retelling of this event, the *Buddhacharita,* the Buddhist historian and philosopher Ashvaghosa gives us a more ample account of that moment under the rose-apple tree.[4] When Gautama was still a young man living in his father's palace, one day he felt disquieted and vaguely depressed. He went on an excursion to the countryside, riding his horse and accompanied by servants. As he slowly rides along, he watches the men working in the fields. Rather unexpectedly, he notices that many small creatures are being killed in the course of plowing:

---

3. *The Middle Length Discourses,* 36.31.
4. I have used the condensed translation of the *Buddhacharita* given by Edward Conze in his *Buddhist Scriptures* (New York: Penguin Books, 1983).

The beauties of the landscape and his longing for the forest carried him deep into the countryside. There he saw the soil being ploughed. Its surface, broken with furrows, looked like rippling water. The ploughs had torn up the sprouting grass, scattering tufts here and there, and the land was littered with tiny creatures who had been killed and injured — worms, insects, and the like. The sight of all this grieved the prince as deeply as if he had witnessed the slaughter of his own kinsmen.

He looks up and notices how hard the lives of the farmers must be:

He observed the ploughmen, saw how they suffered from wind, sun, and dust, and how the oxen were worn down by the labor of drawing.

Seeing all this he is overwhelmed with pity, and he sits down under a rose-apple tree:

In the supreme nobility of his mind he performed an act of supreme pity. Then he got down from his horse and walked gently and slowly over the ground, overcome with grief. He reflected on the birth and passing away of all living things. In his distress he said to himself, "How pitiful is all this!" His mind longed for solitude, he withdrew from the good friends who walked behind him, and went to a solitary spot at the foot of a rose-apple tree. The tree's lovely leaves were in constant motion, and the ground underneath it salubrious and green like beryl.

He sits there and thinks quietly. He begins to see things clearly, just as they are. His pity, his compassion, keeps growing until he has extended his insight to all creatures and realizes that all reality is interconnected:

He sat down under the tree, and reflected on the origination and passing away of all that lives. Then he worked on his mind in such a way that, with this theme as a basis, it became stable and concentrated. When he had won through to mental stability, he was suddenly freed from all desire for sense-objects and from cares of any kind. He had reached the first stage of meditation.... In this state of meditation, he considered the destiny of the world correctly, just as it is: "Pitiful, indeed, that these people who themselves are helpless and doomed to undergo illness, old age, and destruction, should, in the ignorant blindness of their self-intoxication, show so little respect for others who are likewise victims of old age, disease, and death! But now that I have discerned this supreme Dharma, it would be unworthy and unbecoming if I, who am so constituted, should show no respect for others whose constitution is essentially the same as mine."

Ashvaghosa tells us that Gautama next realizes the nature of the world, just as it is:

When he thus gained insight into the fact that the blemishes of disease, old age, and death vitiate the very core of this world, at the same moment he lost all self-intoxication, which normally arises from pride in one's own strength, youth, and vitality. He now was neither glad nor grieved; all doubt, lassitude, and sleepiness disappeared; sensuous excitements could no longer influence him; and hatred and contempt for others were far from his mind.[5]

In other words, he has begun to see clearly the truth of reality. In that early moment, though he did not then appreciate the full significance of what he had discovered, he had effortlessly entered upon the realization which would later blossom into his great enlightenment.

Over the years he had forgotten about the rose-apple tree. To save himself he had to flee to the forest, go through great difficulties, and find himself frustrated by a fruitless, painful search for peace, all before he could begin to remember again. At his moment of failure, he thinks back to that earlier unexpected, unprepared for experience under the rose-apple tree, which once again illumines his way:

It became clear to him that this kind of excessive self-torture merely wore out his body without any useful result. Impelled both by his dread of becoming and by his longing for Buddhahood, he reasoned as follows: "This is not the Dharma which leads to dispassion, to enlightenment, to emancipation. That method which some time ago I found under the rose-apple tree, that was more certain in its results. But those meditations cannot be carried out in this weakened condition; therefore I must take steps to increase again the strength of this body."[6]

---

5. Conze, *Buddhist Scriptures,* 42–43.
6. Conze, *Buddhist Scriptures,* 46.

Because he remembers, he stops his fruitless quest. He rests and begins to recover his health and balance; as it were, he picks up again the thread of realization he had begun to follow years before. Now he can sit under a tree once again, settling down quietly. He enters upon deeper levels of meditation until he remembers his past lives, sees in totality the passing away and reappearing of beings, and realizes the sure path to this steady and liberative remembering and present awareness. Gautama becomes fully awakened; he becomes Buddha.

So much that is so important for the history of Buddhism therefore hinges on the fact that he remembers sitting under that rose-apple tree. The deepest and most sought after experience was there, already, in the beginning, although he did not appreciate where this knowledge might lead him. In the forest his mind becomes clear when he finally realizes that wisdom does not lie in dramatic gestures and heroic efforts at all, but in a quiet awareness that cannot be the product of activity, a simple realization of the way things are.

Telling his story and describing his great quest in the context of remembering the rose-apple tree — all of this is simply part of the Buddha's answer to Sacchaka's questions in sutta 36. Just as years before he had remembered the rose-apple tree at a key moment in his arduous spiritual quest, so now, for Sacchaka's sake, he remembers his quest, again for a liberative purpose. He shares his story in order to illustrate that in themselves pleasure and pain are neither friends nor enemies. It is mind that makes the difference, the problem and its solution are both within us, so there is no point in punishing or pampering the body. He even confesses to Sacchaka that yes, he does nap in the afternoon. Sacchaka offers his thanks and departs; he is a busy man and has other things to do. We do not get the impression that the Buddha has changed Sacchaka's way of thinking and living, but we who read about their encounter are invited to look again at our lives in the mirror of the Buddha and to remember quiet moments when we have already found what we seek. Even if we are more willing than Sacchaka to learn from the Buddha, we need not turn to him for a special teaching. His search and his act of remembering teach us that freedom awaits us when we observe our life just as we have actually been living it, before and now. Remembering is the key to living now, in the present.

All of this may remind us of another account where remembering is key to salvation. At the end of the Gospel according to Luke, after the death of Jesus, two disciples were on the road to Emmaus. They were returning to their village distressed and disappointed, for their hopes had been dashed. Jesus, upon whom they had pinned all their hopes, had been killed, and that seemed to be the end of the story. As they walked down the road, though,

Jesus walks with them, concealed so that they would not recognize him. He asks them to tell him what they are talking about, and in turn they ask, "Are you the only stranger in Jerusalem who does not know what happened there in these days?" (Luke 24:18). Little by little, he reviews with them what they already know from their own tradition, the Law and the Prophets. He helps them to read their tradition with a new eye, in light of the disappointment they had experienced in Jerusalem, and so also to reinterpret the cross. Gradually, as he speaks, they are awakened spiritually, and they have enough sense to invite him to share a meal with them. At table they recognize him as the one they had been mourning:

> As they were coming near to the village to which they were going, he walked ahead as if he were going on. But they urged him strongly, saying, "Stay with us, because it is almost evening and the day is now nearly over." So he went in to stay with them. While he was at the table with them, he took bread, blessed and broke it, and gave it to them. Then their eyes were opened, and they recognized him; and he vanished from their sight. They said to each other, "Were not our hearts burning within us while he was talking to us on the road, while he was opening the scriptures to us?" (Luke 24:28–32)

Perhaps they are the first Christians to discover Jesus in the eucharistic meal, the breaking of the bread. He is remembered in light of Israel's history and sacred tradition, and thus becomes present again. As the Buddha discovered, recovering the past can liberate the present.

THE FRUITS OF REMEMBERING

Though it is rare for the Buddha to tell his story so fully, he frequently teaches that it is spiritually fruitful to remember one's own story and thus see one's life differently. By stories — his own story, what he has heard from of old, and the stories of the people he meets — he helps others to retrieve a sense of their lives, to redeem the present in light of the past. When people remember and take to heart what is already present but unnoticed in their own lives, true liberation becomes possible.

The Buddha skillfully teaches a wide range of people from all backgrounds: a brahmin who assumes without much basis that he knows exactly what it means to be a brahmin; a king who is about to offer an animal sacrifice but who does not understand the meaning of sacrifice; monks who devote themselves to the way of the Buddha but shy away from helping a sick monk; boys who torment a small animal, never thinking to feel sorry for the animal; a leper, suffering for the sins of a past life, who is singled out and taught specially by the Buddha; an infamous murderer who finds salvation in humble suffering. In each case, the Buddha helps the individual to face up to the implications of his or her situation, to find somewhere in experience the strength and wisdom to embrace life now. For example, let us look at just one story of how the Buddha helped someone to take a fresh look at her life.

THE PARABLE OF THE MUSTARD SEED

This beautiful story captures something very basic about life and about how the Buddha understood it:[7]

> Gotami was her family name, but because she was frail, they called her Kisha (Frail) Gotami. She had been reborn at Savatthi into a poverty-stricken house. When she grew up she married and went to her husband's house. But it was only after she gave birth to a son that they treated her with respect. But just when the boy was old enough to play, he died. Sorrow sprang up within her, and she went from house to house looking for some medicine that would bring him back to life. But people laughed at her, saying, "Where can you find medicine for the dead?" Finally, a wise man told her, "Woman, if you wish medicine for your son, go to the possessor of the ten forces, the foremost individual in the world of humans and the world of the gods. He is Gautama, the Buddha, and he dwells nearby. He alone will know the medicine." So she went to where the Buddha was staying. She stood before him and asked him for medicine.

Kisha Gotami goes to the Buddha, and surely he could have given her a discourse on the meaning of death. Instead, he chooses a more practical route that gently guides her to review her own life:

> Seeing that she was ripe for conversion, he said to her, "Go, enter the city, make the rounds of the entire city, and in whichever house no one has ever died, from that house fetch tiny grains of mustard seed." "Very well, sir," she replied, and she went off delighted in heart to look for that mustard seed. But in each house she entered, she found that someone had died: in one, a daughter; in another, a mother in childbirth; in

---

7. This version of the story of Kisha Gotami is slightly adapted from the translation by E. W. Burlingame, *Buddhist Parables* (New Haven: Yale University Press: 1922), 92–94.

a third, a man killed in war. When she had finished going through the city, she had found no house where death had not entered.

Without many words and in a way suited to her need, the Buddha has skillfully guided her to look at the obvious, what is already going on in her own life. She comes to see what she had never noticed before: people are always dying, families are always experiencing loss. Once she sees how close, ordinary, and pervasive death actually is, she stops looking for a personal exemption; her grief is transformed, and she clings no more to her child:

> She exclaimed, "In the entire city this alone is the way of things! The Buddha, filled with compassion for the human race, must have seen this!" Overcome with emotion, she went outside the city and carried her son to the cremation ground. She said to him, "Dear little son, I thought that you alone had been overtaken by this thing which people call death. But you are not the only one death has overtaken, for this is the universal law for all human beings." She returned to the Buddha. He asked her, "O Gotami, did you get that mustard seed?" She replied, "Forget the mustard seed! I understand now what is life and what is death — just give me a place of refuge!" So he taught her; and even as she stood there she became established in the fruit of conversion, and requested admission to the Order. He granted her permission, and she took refuge in the Order.

MASTERS OF LIFE

Even the first time I read this story, I thought immediately of the widow of Nain in the Gospel according to Luke, a story which speaks so simply of Jesus' compassion for the lost and lonely, of hope even at the most desolate of moments:

> Soon afterwards Jesus went to a city called Nain, and his disciples and a great crowd went with him. As he drew near to the gate of the city, behold, a man who had died was being carried out, the only son of his mother, and she was a widow; and a large crowd from the city was with her.

Jesus involves himself in her suffering and radically changes the situation:

When the Lord saw her, he had compassion on her and said to her, "Do not weep." And he came and touched the bier, and the bearers stood still. Jesus said, "Young man, I say to you, arise." The dead man sat up, and began to speak. Jesus gave him to his mother. Fear seized them all, and they glorified God, saying, "A great prophet has arisen among us!" and "God has visited his people!" This report concerning him spread through the whole of Judea and all the surrounding country. (Luke 7:11–17)

Both Jesus and the Buddha console, though in very different ways. It is good for us to hope to become like Jesus who heals, who brings good news and comfort to those in mourning. Yet we would be foolish to avoid being like the Buddha, who uncovers larger, inescapable patterns of life and death that persist in our modern world, where miracles are so rare and mustard seeds so common. We may try to put people in touch with the world as it is, as did the Buddha. Yet we would be foolish to forget that death can be transformed into life, now.

It may be helpful to imagine the quest and enlightenment and teaching of the Buddha as a series of concentric circles, spreading out from his moment under the rose-apple tree, his original graced moment. Because he did not understand that moment, he fled to the forest; because he thought that someone else might have the answer to his problems, he wasted years with teachers; because he failed in his search, he finally remembered that moment in his youth when he had been so very peaceful; because he remembered, he came to understand everything; because he had learned from his life, he could help Kisha Gotami to take a new look at her own village. He could even strip away the layers of hardened opinion by which Sacchaka protected himself and at least offer him a chance to become simple and free again.

The *Great Forest Teaching* and the *Crest Jewel* advise us on how to find and transform the self, and thus to be free. Though the Buddha is remembered as the great teacher of the doctrine of no-self, he helps us to look again at our lives and memories, who we are as persons. He tells us not to yearn for the beginning of time and the creation of the world, and not to despise our present selves during the quest for a better, inner self. But he very much wants us to know who we are and have been, and so to change our way of thinking. If we search our personal stories, we will find moments of clarity and peace already there. It is the gift of those moments, now remembered, that sets us free even in the face of death. We let go of self, we trace the course of our lives, and we become better persons.

That is to say, when we seek wisdom, we should not do so because we despise who we already are or what our own tradition already gives to us. Rather, in that wisdom we will find ways to see ourselves anew, to look again at the place we come from. Hindus and Buddhists alike would agree that there is no forest where we can escape the confusions of life, no book with every answer, no teacher who knows exactly what we should do; by visiting India, though, perhaps we can remember again the rose-apple tree already growing in the center of our garden.

4

Seeing Krishna,
Seeing Everything

In reflecting on the creation myths, the *Crest Jewel,* and even the story of the Buddha, I have stressed that spiritual growth and learning have to be founded in the discovery of self. Without knowledge of myself, just as I really am, nothing more is possible; if I have self-knowledge, nothing else is really necessary for me to be fully alive, here and now. But although religious traditions do speak of self in such terms and even more vigorously, quite often they say something more: they urge their members to turn to God above all else, God who most deeply satisfies the self, God who is the self of the self, God who is the one completely satisfying object of vision.

In the Hindu religious traditions we are frequently and emphatically brought into encounter with God, with gods and goddesses, as the true focus of the greatest desires. If we are to understand the religious heritage of India, we must also reflect on the meaning of the great divinities. In the next three chapters I shall focus on Krishna, Shiva, and the Goddess. Reflection on Krishna will remind us that God offers the deepest fulfillment possible for a human being; reflection on Shiva reminds us that God is always more than we can imagine, and a great surprise to us; reflection on the Goddess reminds us that to know the divine is to know everything there is to know, completely.

To see God is a simple ideal, and one with deep roots; that we can come near to God and encounter God face to face has long been a very powerful ideal in India. That God is great and transcends our ordinary ways of knowing has never meant that God is entirely invisible or inaccessible. In the nineteenth century, for instance, there is Ramakrishna, the remarkable and revered saint who wanted nothing other than to see his Divine Mother, the Goddess Kali, face to face. He was willing to die for the experience, and he almost did. Once, when he was still young, he tried to kill himself in order to remove the barriers which kept him from Kali. He was certainly exceptional, but he spoke for many ordinary Indians when he said this:

> Of course God can be seen and spoken with — just as I am seeing you and speaking with you. But who really wants to see God? To be sure, people grieve and shed many tears at the death of their spouses and children, and some behave that way just for the sake of money and property — but who weeps because they cannot see God?[1]

God is easily seen — if you have eyes to see, if you want it enough, if you cannot bear to live without such vision.

Even Mohandas Gandhi, a pragmatic and busy participant in the everyday world where business and politics were very evident and mysticism seemingly marginal, said that his own religious goal was simply to see God:

> What I want to achieve, — what I have been striving and pining to achieve these thirty years, — is self-realization, to see God face to face, to attain moksa [liberation]. I live and move and have my being in pursuit of this goal.[2]

In his autobiography he recalls that when he was young, one of his most important spiritual guides was a man named Raychandbhai. Gandhi characterizes him as a businessman who wanted nothing more than to see God. Raychandbhai was very good in business,

> but all these things were not the centre around which his life revolved. That centre was the passion to see God face to face. The following lines of Muktanand were always on his lips and engraved on the tablets of his heart: "I shall think myself blessed only when I see him in every one of my daily acts; verily he is the thread which supports Muktanand's life." The man who, immediately on finishing his talk about weighty business transactions, began to write about the hidden things of the spirit could evidently not be a businessman at all, but a real seeker after truth. (*Experiments with Truth,* 76)

In chapters 6 and 7 respectively we shall look again at the religious experiences of Ramakrishna and Gandhi. But even at this point we can

---

1. As cited by Mahendranath Gupta in *The Gospel of Ramakrishna,* trans. Swami Nikhilananda (New York: Ramakrishna Vedanta Center, 1942), 83. I have made slight adaptations.
2. Mohandas K. Gandhi, *The Story of My Experiments with Truth,* trans. Mahadev Desai (New York: Dover Publications, 1983), 8.

acknowledge that "seeing God" is very important and also means different things to different people. Let us sort out a few of these meanings.

When some Hindus talk about seeing God, they mean exactly that: God will come, and I will see God face to face. This is more or less what Lakshmi Ma, a contemporary Bengali woman, seems to have meant when she said this:

> Shiva and Durga, and Shiva and Kali appeared before me. I used to show them to my husband, but he could not see anything. . . . One who has seen the Lord and become mad loses all sense and is not conscious of his belongings. One who has become mad by seeing the Lord can be easily distinguished. He will not concentrate on any worldly objects. He will forget even his close relatives and think only about God.[3]

In chapter 5 we will return briefly to her experience.

But not everyone expects to see God so directly and literally as does Lakshmi Ma. When we speak of seeing God in this life, there are other, subtler meanings to keep in mind. In some of the most ancient Vedic texts, for instance, we hear of seers who composed songs to express what they had personally seen of ultimate reality. These seers are remembered precisely because they put their extraordinary experiences into words that could be passed down by word of mouth from generation to generation. Vision came first and was the source of religious authority; words followed from vision. But it was the words, not the original vision, that were available to later generations, and eventually the words mattered more than the vision behind them. Seeing became a metaphor for wisdom — no longer "sight," but "insight." "To see" came to mean "to understand clearly"; "to see God" came to mean "to understand reality as a whole." This is what happened to the student in the *Crest Jewel* who realized everything all at once; it was as if he had seen God.

Since we can see only what is nearby and unobstructed, for some Hindus vision may suggest nearness; the desire to see God may mean a desire to be near God. For others, seeing God means to appreciate fully the precious truth that is partial, obscure, or sporadic in our ordinary experience; to see God is to see everything altogether, all at once. Still other Hindus understand "seeing God" to mark an ideal situation, where people have a free and intelligent relationship with God, instead of blind submission. If we can see God,

---

3. The words of a Bengali woman, Lakshmi Ma, as reported by June McDaniel in *The Madness of the Saints* (Chicago: University of Chicago Press, 1989), 216–19.

then the relationship is no longer just a question of power or possession. God comes within our view; God is someone we can relate to in freedom, as friends, not slaves.

Insight, nearness, completeness, free relationship: these are some aspects of what people mean when they want to see God. In our world today, seeing God may also be the goal of learning from another religion, and we may explore Hindu wisdom because we want a deeper, fuller experience of God. We may have seen God before, in our own way in our own tradition, but now we want to see more of God, more clearly than before. If so, we must be clear about the kind of knowledge we are expecting — be it an apparition or nearness or free interaction. Moreover: granting that a Hindu manages to see God in a certain way, can I who am not a Hindu learn to see God more clearly by drawing on that Hindu experience?

But such questions are rather abstract, and it is better to see for ourselves by way of examples. In this chapter I wish to examine just one example, what it has meant for Hindus to see Krishna. Krishna is a very popular God who often seems visible or nearly so, and sometimes his devotees find him visible in a very vivid fashion. When Hindus think of Krishna, they are thinking of a God who speaks to the human heart in a language we can understand, a God who appears with a face we can see. As the theologian Ramanuja put it in the eleventh century, Krishna is God — Lord Vishnu, Narayana — come down to this earth so that people can see and hear and touch God.

We will begin with the *Bhagavad Gita* (*The Lord's Song*). Arjuna is a great warrior who stands at the forefront of his family and his army, but now he suffers from an identity crisis. Desperate, he seeks counsel from Krishna, a friend and teacher. We will examine how Arjuna comes closer and closer to Krishna, finally seeing him, and how, in seeing him, he sees more than he really can bear. After that, we will reflect on several other ways of coming near to Krishna, ways which both test and broaden the boundaries set by the *Gita:* Krishna, the handsome youth with the mesmerizing flute; Krishna, the inner joy of every heart; Krishna, the little boy with the charming smile and sparkling eyes.

PEERING INTO GOD'S MOUTH: ARJUNA

The *Bhagavad Gita* is set at the beginning of the great war between the armies of the five Pandava brothers and their hundred cousins. The third brother, Arjuna, is the foremost warrior on the Pandava side. Just before the battle starts, he goes out to survey the two armies and thus prepare himself psychologically for the fighting to come. Contrary to his expectations, though, he is overwhelmed by an awareness of just how awful this war will be: a bloody struggle within one extended family, among brothers and cousins and uncles, teachers and their disciples. Like the young Gautama who rode out and watched the farmers in the fields, Arjuna is deeply troubled by his vision. He looks life in the face and is appalled; paralyzed with grief and sorrow, he slumps to the ground. But like the student in the *Crest Jewel* and like the Buddha in the forest, Arjuna's mind is opened at this moment of crisis. Because Arjuna has real and unanswered questions, he becomes able to learn, and his charioteer, the divine Krishna, becomes his teacher.

Krishna begins to teach, weaving back and forth a series of appeals which push Arjuna to examine his self-image, his traditional values, and his expectations for the future. Arjuna has been mistaken in deriving his identity from his society's values and rules; when society falls into conflict, it is predictable that he suffers a personal crisis. When he worries about death, it is because he is looking in the wrong direction and at things that inevitably pass away, instead of at the true self that never dies:

> Never have I not existed, nor you, nor these rulers, and never in the future shall we cease to exist.... This self is not born, it does not die; having come to be, it will never cease to be; unborn, enduring, constant, and primordial, it is not killed when the body is killed. It cannot be cut or burned; it cannot be wet or withered; it is enduring, all-pervasive, fixed, immovable, there from the beginning. (2.12, 20, 24)[4]

He must look inside himself for the foundations of his identity, and he must refashion his life accordingly, becoming free from the desires and fears which ordinarily prompt people to act:

> But let a person find delight in the self and feel inner joy and pure contentment in the self. Then there is nothing more to be done. He has no stake here in deeds done or undone, nor does his purpose depend on other creatures. (3.17–18)

The person who knows the self lives a detached and balanced life, treating equally the high and the low, profit and loss, life and death. This person acts freely, in complete freedom. In knowing himself more clearly, Arjuna

---

4. Throughout, all translations are those of Barbara Miller, *The Bhagavad Gita: Krishna's Counsel in Time of War* (New York: Bantam Books, 1986), with slight adaptations.

becomes able to get beyond his grief; he can return to his duty, his role in the inevitable war.

The *Gita* seems to imply that Arjuna hears this wisdom from Krishna, takes it to heart, and is changed. As he grows in self-knowledge and detachment, he becomes more able to see reality as a whole and grows in his awareness of Krishna himself. In chapters 9 and 10, Krishna draws Arjuna deeper into his divine mystery. First, he shows Arjuna how everything in the universe depends entirely on himself, Krishna. Though he is transcendent, he is also nearby, present everywhere — throughout the universe, in all living beings, in every religious and social group, in the human heart. To find him, you must simply love him:

> The leaf or flower or fruit or water that a person offers with devotion,
> I take from that person of self-restraint in response to his devotion.
> Whatever you do — what you take, what you offer, what you give, what
> penances you perform — do as an offering to me, Arjuna! (9.26–27)

If you love him, you will notice him everywhere. In chapter 10, Krishna offers a long series of examples which show Arjuna that he is to find Krishna within each particular reality:

> I am the self abiding in the heart of all creatures; I am their beginning,
> their middle, and their end. I am Vishnu striding among the sun gods, I
> am the radiant sun among lights, I am lightning among the wind gods,
> the moon among stars. I am the song in sacred lore; I am Indra among
> the gods; I am the mind of the senses, the consciousness of creatures. I
> am gracious Shiva among the howling storm gods, the Lord of wealth
> among demigods and demons, fire blazing among the bright gods, I am
> Meru among mountains.... Fiery hero, endless are my divine powers,
> my power's extent I have barely hinted. Whatever is powerful, lucid,
> splendid, or invulnerable has its source in a fragment of my brilliance.
> But what use is so much knowledge to you, Arjuna? I stand sustaining
> the entire world with a fragment of my being. (10.20–23, 40–42)

At the beginning of chapter 11, Arjuna finally asks to see Krishna face to face, as he truly is:

> To favor me you revealed the deepest mystery of the self, and by your
> words my delusion is dispelled. I heard from you in detail how crea-
> tures come to be and die, Krishna, and about the self in its immutable

greatness. Just as you have described yourself, I wish to see your form in all its majesty, Krishna, supreme among all people. Krishna, Lord of discipline, if you think I can see it, reveal to me your immutable self! (11.1–4)

Though Arjuna is now as ready as he can be, vision is still a gift; no human being can just decide to look at God, as if God were merely an object for perusal:

Arjuna, see my forms in hundreds and thousands; diverse, divine, of many colors and shapes. See the sun gods, gods of light, howling storm gods, twin gods of dawn, and gods of wind, Arjuna, wondrous forms not seen before. Arjuna, see all the universe, animate and inanimate, and whatever else you wish to see; all stands here as one in my body. But you cannot see me with your own eye; I give you a divine eye to see the majesty of my discipline! (11.5, 7–8)

Thus graced, Arjuna sees more clearly than ever before; he sees everything:

If the light of a thousand suns were to rise in the sky at once, it would be like the light of this great spirit. I see your boundless form everywhere, the countless arms, bodies, mouths, and eyes; Lord of all, I see no end or middle or beginning to your totality. (11.12, 16)

But this wonderful vision of Krishna terrifies him:

When I see the many mouths and eyes of your great form, its many arms, thighs, feet, bellies, and fangs — the worlds tremble and so do I. Vishnu, I see you brush the clouds with flames of countless colors, I see your mouths agape, I see your huge eyes blazing — my inner self quakes and I find no resolve or tranquility. Seeing the fangs protruding from your mouths like the fires of time, I lose my bearings and I find no refuge; be gracious, Lord of gods, shelter of the universe. (11.23–25)

Arjuna stands at the brink of the ultimate experience, where Death and God seem one, where to see God is to die.

The prophet Isaiah expresses something of the same experience:

In the year that King Uzziah died, I saw the Lord sitting on a throne, high and lofty; and the hem of his robe filled the temple. Seraphs were in attendance above him. Each had six wings: with two they covered their faces, with two they covered their feet, and with two they flew. And one called to another and said, "Holy, holy, holy is the Lord of hosts; the whole earth is full of his glory." The pivots on the thresholds shook at the voices of those who called, and the house filled with smoke. And I said, "Woe is me! I am lost, for I am a person of unclean lips, and I live among a people of unclean lips; yet my eyes have seen the King, the Lord of hosts." (Isa. 6:1–5)

Like Isaiah, Arjuna is terrified by his vision of God; he finds himself slipping into dissolution, for he is faced with death, his own death. He cannot remain in so heightened a state if he is to continue living, so he begs to return to ordinary life:

I am thrilled, and yet my mind trembles with fear at seeing what has not been seen before. So show me, God, the form I know — be gracious, Lord of gods, Shelter of the World. I want to see you as before, with your crown and your mace, and the discus in your hand. God with a thousand arms, please assume the four-armed form embodied in your totality. (11.45–46)

For some of us, our encounter with God may begin as it did for Arjuna, in a moment of religious crisis where the ideals of religion no longer seem to fit together, where it no longer seems possible to act religiously in a coherent way. If I remain just as I am, I may be ignoring deeply felt needs and desires; if I change, I may be turning my back on my tradition. Like Arjuna, we can grow spiritually if we keep growing in self-knowledge and in the detachment that follows upon that awareness. Insofar as we find some measure of the inner balance that makes it possible to be vulnerable and open, to keep our eyes open, we will be able to learn from another religion. In beginning to understand what it means for a Hindu to see Krishna as Arjuna does, we broaden the horizons of our own religious experience and allow God to fill our world. In learning the wisdom of the *Gita,* we change, and we begin to see God more clearly, unobstructed by habits and set ideas about who God is.

As we come to know God more deeply, however, we too may find that seeing God is not simply a comfortable experience. To see God is to see everything, the negative as well as the positive, death as well as life, our place and our insignificance. Although our experiments with Hindu wisdom may at first be limited and cautious, in the long run they may turn out to be more than we want: do I really want to know all this about Hinduism, if it fills my head with a thousand new thoughts and pulls my heart in ten directions at once? If this new wisdom is not related to seeing God more clearly, it may not be worth the trouble; if it does help me to see God, I may start seeing God in unfamiliar forms which affect even the way I pray. We may reach the point where going farther seems impossible; we may draw back, hoping to dwell comfortably within our own tradition again. But for Arjuna, the effect is positive; because he has seen Krishna, he now sees everything in perspective; at the end of the *Gita,* he is able to return to his warrior's duty:

> Krishna, my delusion is destroyed, and by your grace I have regained my memory. Here I stand, my doubt dispelled, ready to act on your words. (18.73)

If we learn to see through Arjuna's eyes, we too may begin to see God more clearly; we too may return wiser and stronger to our own ways of being and acting religiously. If we would rather back away, we will have to learn to live with our eyes tightly shut.

SO NEAR WE CAN TOUCH HIM: ANDAL

In our second example, we contemplate the cowherd women (*gopi*s) who were the legendary lovers and devotees of the young Krishna. In turn, they will help us to understand the experience of Andal, the south Indian poet who learned to feel and taste Krishna even when he was absent and she could not see him.

Arjuna was a warrior, and he saw God as a frightening figure of life and death, but cowherd women know little beyond the world of the village; they see God as one of their own, their husband and their child. Arjuna completed his spiritual journey with a direct vision of God; the cowherd women began with immediate experiences of Krishna, and then had to cope with his absence. According to tradition, they danced with Krishna, heard his flute, touched him, and were touched by him. He stood before them; they saw him and loved him without limit. In the person of their leader Radha, union with Krishna seems to have reached even the utmost intimacy. Nevertheless, in the end Krishna leaves them, seemingly forgetting them, perhaps for their own good, for they must learn never to cling to God as they had met him in the past. After that, the women's problem is not how to see God, but how to handle the absence of one they have seen and loved before.

When Krishna departs, the cowherd women try to recover his presence by remembering him vividly. They rehearse the dances they had danced with him; they reenact the famous myths which recount his great deeds in the holy land of Vrindavana:

> Crowds of women, their bodies carefully following Krishna's gestures, moved around Vrindavana, looking for the Lord who had gone elsewhere. Those cowherd women, their hearts wed to Krishna, called aloud to one another, "I am Lord Krishna! See my amorous movements!" One spoke up, "Listen to my song, the song of Krishna!" Another, slapping her arm defiantly in imitation of the Lord, said, "Stop there, wicked demon Kaliya! I am Krishna!" Another cried, "Stay here without fear, cowherds. Do not be afraid of the storm!" And still another woman, mimicking Krishna's sport, spoke up, "I have struck down the demon Dhenuka, so let your cows wander where they will!" Thus imitating Krishna's various exploits did the distracted cowherd women cavort in delightful Vrindavana. (*Bhagavata Purana* X)[5]

As they act out these scenes, the women's consciousness is transformed; they find themselves once again near to Krishna for a moment.

Traditionally, the deeds of the cowherd women are meant to be imitated by others, even those who have never actually seen Krishna. God can be approached and experienced if we remember, imagine, and allow ourselves to become actors in the drama of God's work on earth; as they play their parts devotees find, to their surprise and delight, that God comes and interacts with them too, in ways old and new. Such acts of remembering and imagining are very powerful, for they make it possible to experience anew God's mighty deeds from the past. This is surely at the heart of what Jews mean in celebrating the Passover, and Christians in the eucharistic memorial of the death and resurrection of Jesus.

The ninth-century Tamil-language poet Andal relived the experiences of the cowherd women in a more "ordinary time" in which miracles and divine apparitions recede to the distant past, in which God is not present in any supernatural way. Andal's world seems to be a world of religious stability, devotion, and moderate piety. God can be experienced in predictable and ordinary ways simply by visiting a temple or hearing a holy story, though not with the intense feeling that comes from seeing God directly, being touched by God.

---

5. Drawn from an excerpt from the *Bhagavata Purana,* trans. Cornelia Dimmitt and J. A. B. van Buitenenen in *Classical Hindu Mythology* (Philadelphia: Temple University Press, 1978), 121. The tenth book of the *Bhagavata Purana* tells the life story of Krishna, his deeds and encounters on earth.

Like the cowherd women, Andal very much wanted to see; she drew on
their tradition in order to deepen her own experience of Krishna and put
her longing into words. In the first of her two works, *Tiruppavai* (*The Song
of Our Vow*), she evokes what was probably already an old custom, young
women going to the river on winter mornings to bathe in cold water and by
such penance either to win husbands or entreat God to come to them directly.
The young women move from house to house through the village, waking up
more young women in succession, their numbers growing:

> Silly child, don't you hear the noisy chatter of blackbirds filling the
>   morning air,
> the jingle of necklaces which the women of our town wear in their
>   fragrant hair?
> Don't you hear the swish of buttermilk as the churning rod moves to
>   and fro?
> Fine girl, how can you sleep while we stand here singing the glories of
>   Narayana who has come to us as Keshava?
> Bright girl, rise from your sleep, open your door.
> Such is our winter vow. (*Tiruppavai* 7)[6]

As Andal's song progresses through its thirty verses, the young women
reach Krishna's house; they meet the members of his household and his wife,
and finally come into his presence. Standing before him, they rouse him from
sleep, hoping he will look directly at them:

> Like the kings of this lovely wide world
>   who come and break their pride
>   by gathering at the foot of your couch,
> we lay our heads there;
> will you not let fall upon us even a little your bright eye
> which is like the lotus flower,
> just opening as if the slit in a kinkini bell?
> If you look upon us with your lovely eyes
> that are like the moon and the sun rising together,
> the curse on us will fall away:
> such is our winter vow. (*Tiruppavai* 22)

---

6. Andal's verses are cited with slight adaptations from the translation by Vidya Dehejia,
Antal and Her Path of Love: Poems of a Woman Saint from South India (Albany: State University
of New York Press, 1990).

In the end, they find in him everything they had been seeking:

> At the break of dawn we rise to serve you Krishna,
> we worship at your feet.
> Great indeed is our fortune: born in our cowherd clan,
> you cannot deny us, you are bound to accept our little services.
> Krishna, we do not come to ask for that ritual drum as our prize.
> We are your servants, we serve only you,
> forever and a day we shall be connected with you.
> Let all our desires be transformed now.
> Such is our winter vow. (*Tiruppavai* 29)

To wake up, to come near, and finally to see and be seen: *Tiruppavai* draws on these simple experiences to tell us what finding God is all about.

In her *Nacchiyar Tirumoli* (*The Lady's Holy Words*) Andal more intensely explores Krishna's presence and absence in words that are both playful and terribly intense. She sings about the time when he came and flirted with them, kicking over sandcastles they were building, about a game she and the other girls played — closing their eyes and drawing circles to divine whether Krishna would come or not — and about sending even the birds as her messengers to him. She describes in vivid detail how she once dreamt of marrying Krishna. But still he does not come, and she gives voice to her anguish:

> I hunger and thirst for a sight of Krishna, my dark Lord,
> so don't stand there mocking me, friends!
> Your words sting like sour juice poured on an open wound.
> Go, bring me the yellow silk wrapped around the waist
> of the One who does not understand the sorrow of women,
> fan me with it, cool the burning of my heart.
>
> I weep, I sing his glories, but he does not show me his form,
> he does not say, "Have no fear," he does not come close,
> he does not caress me nor embrace me, he does not fill me up.
> Through the leafy pastures where his cows graze
> the sound of the flute played by the tall Lord reaches me:
> go, bring me cool nectar from the lips of that flute,
> spread it over my face — that will revive me.
>
> (*Nacchiyar Tirumoli* 13.1, 5)

She still cannot see him, but she makes up for this by anticipating the cool breeze she will feel when she is fanned by his cloak; the saliva from the lip of his flute, rubbed all over her face, will be good enough for now. If she cannot see him, she wants only to be held by him:

> All the worlds exalt this one
> who flies the victory banner of the Eagle
> — but it seems his mother reared him
> just like the bitter margosa tree, to serve no purpose.
> To wipe away the sorrow of these innocent breasts,
> the sorrow of not finding him,
> hold them tight against his youthful shoulders,
> bind them there! (*Nacchiyar Tirumoli* 13.7)

Vision is painful and the lack of vision a torment; but the nearness of taste and touch makes it possible to continue living when he seems far away.

We might compare Andal's experience with that of similar great mystics in other religious traditions. Teresa of Avila, a Christian contemplative nun, writes in this way about how intensely she thirsted for God:

> For the soul thirsts no more for the things of this world, although its craving for the next life exceeds any natural thirst that can be imagined. Yet how the heart pines for this very thirst, realizing its priceless value.... When it has been satiated by God, one of the great graces God can bestow on the spirit is to leave it with this thirst which, after drinking, increases the longing to partake again and again of this water. This love and desire of God may increase until nature can bear it no longer — people have died because of this. I know someone to whose aid God came promptly with such abundance of this living water that she was almost drawn out of herself in raptures. Her thirst and growing desire were such that she realized it was quite possible to die of such longing, were it not remedied.[7]

Seeing and tasting are alike in the sense that each brings the lover near to the beloved: vision promises face-to-face encounter; taste indicates that one ends up inside the other, consumed as it were: "Taste and see that the Lord is good; happy are those who take refuge in the Lord" (Ps. 34:8).

If we want to see God within our own religious tradition or across religious boundaries, we have to be thirsty, to imagine and yearn and awaken in God's presence, as did Andal and the cowherd women. Like them, we may

---

7. Teresa of Avila, *The Way of Perfection,* trans. F. Benedict Zimmerman (London: Baker, 1925), chap. 19.

have to remember how God has worked in the past, and thus become able to recognize God working again in our lives too. We can meet God in what is new if we can remember where God has already been at work.

Arjuna's ascetic path of detachment is not for everyone, so it is good that there are alternative paths, imaginative, playful, dramatic practices such as those of the cowherd women. Learning the wisdom of other religions can be as imaginative and heartfelt as we can bear. For some this learning is a path of intense intellectual concentration; for others, it is a dance, an embrace, even a mingling of souls. Sometimes body itself may seem a large problem: we can't find God where we happen to live; we can't see God with these physical eyes. But Andal shows us that having a body is our last slender hope when we are looking for a God who seems far away. To see and hear, to touch and taste, or to be deprived of all these — such are the experiences which intensify our longing for God; even our hungers announce the arrival of God. In learning from other religions, at times our minds may leave us cold and distant. We do well then to follow what attracts us and moves us deeply, even if we cannot understand what is happening or why it should be so. If we find ourselves reminded of God in some gentle whisper or devoted act or simple image, that is enough, for we can begin our journey to where God is from there. Andal turned absence into a palpable experience of God; if we cannot see God yet, our desire itself may become the place to find God very near.

GOD SEES US FIRST: SHATAKOPAN

Shatakopan, another south Indian poet saint, was probably a contemporary of Andal in the ninth century. Like Andal, he too searched for God and seems to have been consumed by his desire to see God. In the hundred songs (1102 verses) of his great *Tiruvaymoli* (perhaps best translated as *The Holy Word of Mouth*) he explores the human desire for God and the possibilities of getting to see God in this life. From many angles he savors the glimpses of God he has received earlier in life, the passing moments in which God seems very near or very far off; again and again, he seeks more of God.[8]

Though we know very little about him beyond the poems attributed to him, it is helpful to recall what the tradition tells us about the extraordinary interior event and inner vision expressed in his songs. When Shatakopan was born, they say, he refused to eat or drink; finally his concerned parents

---

8. Shatakopan is more popularly known as Nammalvar, "our saint." I have explored *Tiruvaymoli* and the traditional view of Shatakopan in my book *Seeing through Texts: Doing Theology among the Srivaisnavas of South India* (Albany: State University of New York Press, 1996).

entrusted this strange boy to God, leaving him under a tamarind tree at a temple. He sat there for sixteen years, deep in meditation, struggling to focus and maintain his desire to see God in a world where God seems invisible. These verses suggest how eager he was to savor Vishnu's great deeds in the past and to await his coming anew:

> I worship you again and again, joining my hands all day long,
> without a moment's rest, lofty one reclining on your bed, the hooded
>   snake!
> My eyes truly wish to see you.

> I wonder, "Will he come and appear before my eyes?"
> and I hear the faint sound of the soaring eagle who rejoices
> when the dwarf who held the earth mounts him.
> My ears wait, I think steadily.

> I taste again the honey of past times, and songs, fruit of praise, fill my
>   ears;
> your broad golden discus rules this earth, my life desires you inces-
>   santly.

> "My life, full ambrosia, you rule me from your winged eagle, holding
>   your radiant discus!"
> Though this sinner's heart thus cries out and calls for a long time,
> Still I have not glimpsed your beauty.

> "Dark blue beauty, lotus eyes, good one who splits me in two,
> my past, present and future!"
> When will I get to see you?

> Great one, you passed between those two great fine trees;
> I grieve, confused, longing to see your feet:
> how long must I be patient, calling out to you with this garland of
>   songs? (*Tiruvaymoli* III.8.4, 5, 7, 8, 10)[9]

As he searches, though, he realizes that the God he seeks had already been at work in his life, from the beginning. To explain this, he recalls the famous myth in which Lord Vishnu came to earth as a dwarf. The haughty demon King Bali thought nothing of it when the dwarf asked him for three steps of earth, for he did not recognize the dwarf as the Lord of the universe. When

---

9. All translations from *Tiruvaymoli* are drawn from my unpublished translation of the whole work.

Bali gave the three steps, Vishnu returned to his cosmic size, measuring the entire earth and sky and heavens with his steps; some versions of the myth say that in his third step he put his foot on the head of the chastened Bali, who became his devotee. In the same way, just like that, God slipped unnoticed into Shatakopan's life, small at first, but gradually taking it all for himself:

> In that time when I did not know you, you made me love your service,
> in the midst of my unknowing confusion, you made me your servant;
> disguised as a dwarf, you asked,
> "Three steps of earth, great King Bali," and you tricked him unawares
> and now you've mingled inside my self. (*Tiruvaymoli* II.3.3)

Shatakopan struggles to balance three things: his sense of God's presence, his deep need to see God more directly, and the apparent impossibility of seeing God here, while in the body. At times he seems lost; at other times he seems overwhelmed by his vision of God. For instance, the following verses recount the holy distraction of a young woman who went to a temple with her friends and thereafter could think of nothing but her lord whom she had seen in the inner sanctum of the temple at Tolaivillimangalam:

> After seeing Tolaivillimangalam
> where people dwell who prosper in the lasting four Vedas,
> she's lost all self-control, see, she's beyond you, women;
> she cries, "Lord Krishna, dark as the sea, is everything that can be learned!"
> She has no modesty left, she keeps rejoicing, delighted within
> she melts away.
>
> The poor thing, she melts, her face shines, for after entering Tolaivillimangalam
> you showed her the Lord with the red lotus eyes, the splendid light;
> starting then, her eyes have rained like clouds, she is amazed, women,
> her mind has gone inside there, she keeps on looking in that direction, worshiping.
>
> Everywhere you see sugar cane, tall ripening paddy, luxuriant red lotuses
> at rich Tolaivillimangalam on the north bank of the cool Porunal River;
> after seeing this she looks nowhere but that direction, all day, every day,

and the only word in her mouth is the name of the jewel colored one,
   women. (*Tiruvaymoli* VI.5.4–6)

These verses speak of longing, discovery, the inability to forget. We sense
that Shatakopan has glimpsed God many times over but cannot hold on to
these fleeting experiences, nor adjust the rest of his life to what he has seen.
Nanjiyar, an early commentator, puts it this way:

> When Shatakopan experiences even one of the Lord's qualities, his
> abundant pleasure in this quality makes him unable to desire any
> lesser object, and makes him desire the Lord's other qualities all the
> more. His desire increases, so that he can no longer settle for grasping
> these qualities one by one, instead of all at once. He grieves to lose
> even a small part of what he desires, even the smallest particle of his
> experience of the Lord, due to factors like weakness of memory, etc.[10]

The commentators say that *Tiruvaymoli* records Shatakopan's quest to see
God; it is the fruit of his frustration and periodic glimpses of God. Ultimately, they say, he fails to devise a foolproof way of seeing God and has
to concede that vision is not something he can make happen. In a climac-
tic verse about two-thirds of the way through *Tiruvaymoli,* Shatakopan gives
up relying on himself and throws himself down at the feet of the Lord who
dwells in the great temple in Venkatam:

> "I cannot be away from you even for a moment," says the Maiden on
>   the flower who dwells on your chest;
> You are unmatched in fame, owner of the three worlds, my Ruler,
> O Lord of holy Venkatam where peerless immortals and crowds of
>   sages delight:
> with no place else to go, this servant has entered right beneath your
>   feet. (*Tiruvaymoli* VI.10.10)

Like the Buddha, Shatakopan admits that nothing he has done really works;
his answer is to surrender before God, completely and without condition. He
falls on his face at the Lord's feet because he is finally giving up his quest to
work things out by himself. The commentators see this surrender as a great
act of substitution: since he cannot see God directly, Shatakopan seizes on
the immediacy of being very near to God, beneath his feet, near enough to
touch and be touched.

---

10. From my translation of Nanjiyar's introduction to *Tiruvaymoli.*

The tradition says that after this song of surrender there is silence before the next song. The saint has done all that he can and now has to wait for a response from the Lord. The Lord then seems to have a change of heart, and he shows a side of himself which Shatakopan had not realized previously: the Lord wants to see Shatakopan — if he gives up his restless activity he will be able to let the Lord do what he wants, to come racing after him.

The remaining songs of *Tiruvaymoli* tell us how the saint is pursued by God. At the end of *Tiruvaymoli,* the tradition says, Shatakopan finally leaves his body behind after affirming not so much a vision of God as an embrace; he is immersed in God:

> Surrounding, entering, filling, raising Nature beyond limit;
> surrounding that and greater still, the highest light;
> surrounding that and greater still, fiery knowledge and bliss;
> surrounding that and greater still, my love for you;
> surrounding that, you finish me,
> surrounding me. (*Tiruvaymoli* X.10.10)

He is so close he cannot see God anymore.

That God first seeks us and permeates our hearts is perhaps what St. Augustine had in mind when he expressed his experience of God by remembering how God had already been present in his life:

> Truly you dwell in my memory, since I have remembered you from the time I learned of you, and I find you there when I call you to mind. Too late have I loved you, O Beauty so ancient and so new, too late have I loved you! Behold, you were within me, while I was outside. It was there that I sought you and, a deformed creature, I rushed headlong upon these things of beauty which you have made. You were with me, but I was not with you.... You have called to me, and have cried out, and have shattered my deafness. You have blazed forth with light, and have shone upon me, and you have put my blindness to flight. You have sent forth fragrance, and I have drawn in my breath, and I pant after you. I have tasted you, and I hunger and thirst after you. You have touched me, and I have burned for your peace. (*Confessions* X.25, 27)[11]

When we go looking for God in religious traditions other than our own, we may have to realize that we get nowhere on our own. We may have to

---

11. As translated by John K. Ryan in the *Confessions* (Garden City, N.Y.: Image Books, 1960).

give up the quest for a foolproof way to see God; neither our own religion, nor another, nor a grand combination of the two will guarantee that we find God. Instead, Shatakopan might suggest, we need to stop and ponder how it is that God seeks us first; it is God who finds us at home, in our own traditions, and it is God who meets us on the road when we go forth. God is always there first, looking for us.

SEEING KRISHNA IN EVERYDAY LIFE: YASHODA

Finally, we consider Yashoda, Krishna's village mother when he was a child; in contrast with Arjuna, Andal, and Shatakopan, she seems to find God simply and easily. Many stories about the youthful, playful Krishna emphasize that he was a typical boy: attractive, happy, naughty, unpredictable, yet always a delight to his mother. Yashoda delights in her son; they are always together. She loves her God as a mother loves her child. God is always and easily nearby, a cherished part of ordinary life; she does not have to search for God or the meaning of life. She simply dotes upon her little boy, and that is enough. But the unexpected still intrudes in the midst of this ordinary way of devotion:

> One day when Krishna and the other boys were playing, they reported to Yashoda, Krishna's mother, "Krishna has been eating dirt!" Yashoda took Krishna by the hand and scolded him, for his own good. Seeing that his eyes seemed bewildered with fear, she said to him, "Naughty boy, why have you secretly eaten dirt? These boys, your friends, and your elder brother, say you have." Krishna replied, "Mother, I have not eaten dirt. They are lying! If you think they speak the truth, look into my mouth yourself." She said to her son, "If that's what you want, then open your mouth."[12]

Arjuna just wanted to see Krishna but ended up peering into the face of infinite reality. Likewise, Yashoda does not know what will happen when she peers into the little mouth of her son, Krishna, Hari:

> So the Lord Hari, the God of unchallenged sovereignty, who in sport had taken the form of a human child, opened his mouth, and Yashoda looked inside. Inside his mouth Yashoda saw the whole eternal universe, and heaven, and the regions of the sky, and the orb of the

---

12. The story of Yashoda and Krishna is found in Book X of the *Bhagavata Purana;* I have used the translation by O'Flaherty in *Hindu Myths,* 220–21, with slight adaptations.

earth with its mountains, islands, and oceans. She saw the wind, and lightning, and the moon and stars, and the whole zodiac.... She saw everything within the body of her son Krishna, inside his mouth, the whole world in all its detail, every form and every living thing and time and nature and action and hope too, and her own village, and even herself.

Like Arjuna, she too is disoriented, and she too surrenders:

She became afraid and confused, thinking, "Is this a dream or an illusion wrought by some god? Do my eyes deceive me? Or is this some portent of the innate powers of this little boy, my son? I bow down at the feet of God whose nature cannot be imagined or grasped by mind, heart, act, or word, who is impossible to fathom, in whom this entire universe rests, I take refuge in God...

She cannot survive in so heightened a state of awareness, so Krishna draws her back down to ordinary maternal consciousness, though with a love that is deepened:

When the cowherd's wife had come to understand reality in this way, Krishna once more spread over her his amazing power, in the guise of maternal affection. Instantly Yashoda lost her memory of what had occurred and took her son onto her lap. She was again as she had been before, but her heart was flooded with an even greater love. She considered Hari — whose greatness is extolled by all the Scriptures, by the three Vedas and all the Upanishads...once more simply her son. (*Bhagavata Purana* X.8)

The story of Yashoda is charming, and it is also relevant for us. We need to respect the heroic quests which often characterize the path to spiritual wisdom, the great confrontations with life and death. But it would be a mistake to confine wisdom to heroic circumstances. Yashoda's example suggests that we do not need the extraordinary and the exotic; ordinary religious practice, persevering love in ordinary duties and relationships, can be the vehicle of divine presence and provide the opportunity for unexpected encounters with God. Life itself is infused with divine presence; the details of ordinary life can become the occasion for moments of vision.

We can compare her experience with the Gospel scene where Jesus is transfigured before several of his disciples, his glory manifest in ordinary time:

> Now about eight days after these sayings Jesus took with him Peter and John and James, and went up on the mountain to pray. And while he was praying, the appearance of his face changed, and his clothes became dazzling white.... Now Peter and his companions were weighed down with sleep; but since they had stayed awake, they saw his glory ... and a cloud came and overshadowed them; and they were terrified as they entered the cloud. Then from the cloud came a voice that said, "This is my Son, my Chosen — listen to him!" When the voice had spoken, Jesus was found alone. (Luke 9:28–32, 34–36)

Like the other apostles, Peter, James, and John were ordinary people who followed Jesus faithfully, sharing his life on a day-to-day basis. They seem to have expected nothing and done nothing special to prepare for his transformation on the mountain. But they were faithful, and they wanted to be with him every day, so they were present when the voice spoke and the light shone.

Patient waiting and daily fidelity are virtues we should cultivate in our spiritual quests, since wisdom takes time. We ought not to turn impatiently to other religions to find there what we could not find in our own tradition. God may not be far away; perhaps God is hiding right where we already are. And when we start investigating other traditions, it will still be important to be patient and faithful in the small details. We may spend years reading Hindu texts and learn many small things in many small ways, without any single great insight. There is wisdom in Yashoda's patient and faithful enjoyment of what is given to her, and as we learn we should allow ourselves to delight in the small bits of wisdom that come our way. Then, like Yashoda, we will be ready for extraordinary encounters and realizations that may come to us. Then one day that richness may be multiplied a thousandfold in a more amazing realization of God.

All of this too is a matter of self-knowledge, getting clear on who we are as we seek God. Arjuna's quest for self-knowledge and stability in life's duties culminates in a life-fulfilling and life-threatening vision of God; for some of us, his combination of duty and self-understanding and vision may be the best entrance into Hindu wisdom. Others among us may live with a palpable sense that God has already touched our lives, before; if so, we need to devote ourselves to recovering those precious moments when times are desolate, as does Andal. Some of us are like Shatakopan, weaving together many strands of wisdom in our search for God. Like him, we may have to learn to welcome even those precious moments of failure when we realize that we cannot make God visible by our own efforts, and we too may come to realize that God loves us first. Perhaps we are all to some extent like Yashoda: living the spiritual life will most usually be a simple, domestic affair, a matter of cherishing God already present in our lives, until something more happens to us. But for all of us, the end will be the same: when we see God, we need nothing else; nothing else is possible.

5

Surprised by Shiva

We must search for self and we must let go of self; these are essential elements of Hindu wisdom. We must look at ourselves in God, for God is the perfect completion of everything we long for, the object of our deepest desire, in whom we come to see our true face, the self of our self.

Yet Hindu wisdom has still more to offer, since God is always more than we can expect, beyond our imagining and beyond the boundaries of our religious understanding; God is there at the edge, even contrary to what we expect, even in what seems improper and improbable. God is more than I can desire. Or, as some Hindus would put it, if we are to understand God fully, we must also encounter Shiva.

Shiva is another of the great gods of Hinduism. He is Shiva, "the benevolent one," but he is also Rudra, "one who howls," terrifying us. Shiva is an ancient figure, but in the oldest traditions he is peripheral, left to one side or simply unmentioned. He was probably not a secure member of the old pantheon of gods which dominates the Vedas; he may have seemed unimportant or weird and offensive to the people who honored the religion of the Vedas and Upanishads. Only later would he be accepted as one of the familiar and greater gods. But even then his original marginal status seemed to stay with him; however society might accept and explain his role, he would always remain mysterious, free from fixed rules and definitions.

In the oldest collection of hymns known as the *Rig Veda,* we find a few mentions of the Rudra who is the disturbing precursor of the relatively more gentle Shiva. Rudra is an outsider God dwelling in the forest, at the margins of the civilized world. This song vividly evokes the image of a long-haired one who follows Rudra:

Long-hair holds fire, holds the drug, holds sky and earth.
Long-hair reveals everything; so that everyone can see the sun, Long-
    hair declares the light.

These ascetics, swathed in wind, put on dirty rags. When gods enter
them, they ride with the rush of the wind:
"Crazy with asceticism, we have mounted the wind.
Our bodies are all you mere mortals can see!"
He sails through the air, looking down on all the shapes below. The
ascetic is friend to this god and that god, devoted to everything done
well.
He is the stallion of the wind, friend of gales lashed on by gods; he is
the ascetic living on two seas, in the east and the west.
He moves with the motion of heavenly girls and youths and wild
beasts.
Long-hair, reading their minds, is their pleasure, their most exciting
friend.
The wind has churned it up; Hunchback prepared it for him; Long-hair
drinks from the cup, he shares the drug with Rudra.[1]

Like Long-hair, Rudra is unpredictable; he is not easily tamed. There is a
famous myth which describes him as both the creator and the destroyer, even
at almost the same time. It seems that once he submerged himself beneath the
ocean and began creating the world through meditation. But when he rose up
from the ocean with his creation, he saw that a demon had been performing
sacrifices in order to make an alternate creation. Rudra became angry, and
he destroyed that demonic creation completely. Though he is the continuing
source of life, he always keeps destroying demon worlds too. Indeed, the
entire cycle and rhythm of life and death is his, for he is both male and
female, Fire together with Soma (the intoxicating herb we encountered in
chapter 2), the beginning and end of everything that is or will be. Because he
is eternally in motion, he is portrayed in art as Nataraja, the Lord of dance;
because he is simple, spare and unmoving, his sign is, as we shall see, a
plain bare column, the lingam.

Meeting Shiva can be like meeting Krishna, because in Shiva too one
finds every deepest hope and longing satisfied; yet to meet Shiva is also
to find that God is shocking, frightening, disturbing. Shiva tests the willingness of devotees to be completely open in encountering God. For us, to
learn from the Hindu experience of Shiva is likewise a double project. It
is to meet an all-encompassing God, the beginning and end of reality, the
source for all religious meaning. But it is also to meet the Lord of all contradictions, a Lord who is more than humans can comprehend, who does not

---

1. *Rig Veda* 10.136, taken, with slight adaptations, from the translation by Wendy D.
O'Flaherty in *Rig Veda* (New York: Penguin, 1981).

fit mental categories, however refined they may be. Shiva destroys all false creations, reminding us that God is never quite what we have determined God to be.

In this chapter I will introduce Shiva through an extended consideration of just one chapter from a text more than a thousand years old, the *Brahmanda Purana,* the myth of "Shiva in the Pine Forest." In this myth Shiva comes to visit some pious ascetics, scandalizes them and shocks them out of their fixed expectations; in the end he also gives them everything they could ever hope for. Though there are no formal divisions in the text, I will present it as a drama in three acts.[2]

ACT ONE: SHOCKED BY GOD

In "Act One" — entitled perhaps "Shocked by God" — we are first introduced to the pious sages who have retired to the forest to perform admirable acts of asceticism:

> Formerly, in the Golden Age, brahmin sages lived on an auspicious peak of the Himalayas, in a delightful pine forest filled with a variety of trees and vines. Numerous sages were practising asceticism there, having taken the vows of the wise. Some ate nothing but moss, others lay down immersed in water; some had clouds as their only shelter, others stood endlessly on the tip of one big toe; some used their teeth for mortars, others broke things on stones; some sat in yogic positions, others took pleasure in living like wild animals. Thus these men of great minds spent their time in keen asceticism.

These are serious penances, indeed, not to be undertaken by the weak-hearted. As in the time of the Buddha, the forest was recognized as a sure refuge to which seekers could retreat to engage in quiet meditation, disciplined methods of physical and mental concentration, and harsh penances meant to subdue body, mind, and spirit. In our myth, these heroic acts are performed by pious sages living a well-ordered forest existence; what might have been admirable penances seem to have been reduced to stylized virtue.

---

2. *Brahmanda Purana* 1.2.27. Throughout, I have used with slight adaptations the translation given by O'Flaherty in *Hindu Myths,* 141–49, but I have also consulted and on occasion preferred the translation by Ganesh V. Tagare given in the series Ancient Indian Tradition and Mythology, vol. 22 (New Delhi: Motilal Banarsidass, 1973). Tagare gives the full hymns of praise excerpted by O'Flaherty.

Virtuous all their lives, these sages now live in seclusion with their wives, intent upon perfecting virtue during their retirement years; they work hard, and are proud of it too.

Shiva comes to them in order to show grace in a typically unusual way:

Then God came to that forest in order to show his grace to them. His body was pale with ashes smeared on it; he was naked, and all the marks by which one might identify him were removed; his hair was disordered and loose; he had enormous pointed teeth; his hands held fire-brands, his eyes were red and tawny; his penis and testicles were like red chalk, his face too ornamented with red and white chalk. Sometimes he laughed horribly; sometimes he sang, smiling; sometimes he danced erotically; he yelled again and again. As he was dancing, the wives of those sages were bewitched and stood in his way as he came into the hermitage begging for alms again and again. The God's wife took a similar form, adorned with ornaments made of grass. He roared like a bull and bellowed like an ass. Thus he began to deceive all the embodied creatures there, laughing at them. The sages grew angry and were overwhelmed by fury....

Wild, naked, obscene: Shiva fits none of the sages' familiar religious categories; he does not exemplify the regular habits to which they have grown accustomed, of which they highly approve. They grow furious at this perceived insult and threat to religious propriety and turn against the stranger:

Deluded by Shiva so that they did not recognize him, the sages said to one another, "This is not the right behavior respected by householders like us, nor is it the conduct of those who delight in chastity, nor of those who live in the forest, nor is this even the righteousness of ascetics. This behavior has never been seen anywhere. Very evil conduct has deluded this fellow. This is not a right way to act for sages and ascetics."

Shiva is the very model of immorality, the vice they left behind in the world but have not forgotten. They are most disturbed by his flagrant nakedness, his exposed penis — his lingam — so they respond with that very intense anger in which sages excel. Their pent-up virtue spews forth in fiery anger, as they curse him:

May that lingam fall off! Speak properly, wear some garment. After your lingam has fallen off, then we will honor you.

Shiva lets them have their way and allows his lingam to fall to the ground. Then he simply departs, without a word. They get exactly what they asked for, though they do not understand what that was. After he leaves,

> there was no further manifestation of divinity among all beings in the triple world, and there was confusion everywhere. Nothing shone forth, the sun gave no heat, purifying fire had no luster.... The sages tried to practice righteousness free from egoism and possessiveness, but their virile powers and their energies were destroyed.

The world has become cold and dark, and they are now impotent, unable to prove their virtue in deeds.

INTERLUDE: WHAT WE LEARN FROM SHIVA'S MAD WAYS

This "first act" of the drama is helpful to us as we think about the relation between conventional ways of being religious and what is different and unfamiliar. In part, this has to do with Shiva himself. As we have already seen, he is the God of opposites; he is not supposed to fit the normal pattern of religious life. His encounter with the sages represents his historical and theological contrariness in dramatic fashion. He is a naked ascetic who is the supreme lord of desire; he is a recluse who intrudes upon reclusive sages; he is full of power, yet lets it fall away in a moment. That Shiva is in some way shocking will be familiar to most Hindus, but even they may find the details of this encounter unsettling. Let us sort out some aspects of its meaning.

The Indian tradition has long recognized that saints can be strange, even mad. People can be possessed by a deity or so overwhelmed by their God-experience that they cannot function normally. Some move to the edge of society in order to express and preserve singular spiritual experiences. They may live in ways that are shocking to the larger population but, if their madness is seen to have religious causes, room is usually made for them. Recall, for instance, this self-description of Lakshmi Ma, the Bengali woman to whom I referred briefly at the beginning of chapter 4:

> Shiva and Durga, and Shiva and Kali appeared before me. I used to show them to my husband, but he could not see anything.... Everyone

thought that I was possessed by evil spirits, so they called an exorcist who bound me with ropes and started burning me. For seven days this continued, but I didn't die, because I had the blessings of Mother. I still have the marks of the burning on my body. Then they bound me in my room, and bound me with thick, iron chains. But I was so powerful that I would break the locks and chains, and go to the temples of Shiva and Mother Kali.

My husband was very good. He used to find me where I had gone and bring me back home. He would give me food to eat. Gradually, I started having matted hair. First I had six knots, but my in-laws forcibly cut them off. Then I became mad, I had no sense. I used to open all my garments, to tear them off and tie them on my head. I rarely ate. I remained in this state for many years. They had cut my matted hair off several times, and I grew insane each time, but now it has grown again, and now I am sensible.... One who has seen the Lord and become mad loses all sense and is not conscious of his belongings. One who has become mad by seeing the Lord can be easily distinguished. He will not concentrate on any worldly objects. He will forget even his close relatives and think only about God.[3]

Encountering certain gods and goddesses goes together with acting in highly unusual ways, and Shiva certainly is one of these gods. This spiritual madness shadows the edges of ordered social organization and shows that a perfect, entirely predictable social order cannot be achieved; neither God nor the religious person can be relied on to be so smoothly rational. Though religion inevitably takes on regular forms, it can never be perfectly sealed off against unpredictable impulses which violate its set standards. Neither God nor God's mad devotees will allow this.

Some religious sects seem to have formed in order to share and stylize religious madness, so that their members might be immune to the pressure of social norms and become more like Shiva. The *Pashupata Sutram* is an ancient text which describes the expected life of such devotees of Shiva.[4] Here I will touch on just a few points made in the text to give a sense of how one community sought to define a life-style appropriate to devotees of the mysterious Shiva.

The ascetic devotee of Shiva in the Pashupata community may be an out-

---

3. *The Madness of the Saints,* 216–19.
4. *Pasupata Sutram with the Pancartha-Bhasya of Kaundinya,* trans. Haripada Chakraborti (Calcutta: Academic Publishers, 1970).

sider to ordinary society, but nevertheless he — it is usually a "he," for it was considered rare and difficult for a woman to take up a socially marginal position — is governed by rules which define his outsider's position. For example: he should bathe in ashes three times a day; he should lie down in ashes when he rests; he should bear marks of Shiva such as ash and garlands; he should live in a solitary place; he should worship Shiva with laughter, songs, dance, loud sounds, salutations to God, whispered prayers, acts of reverence; he should wear only one garment or go about naked; he should avoid being near impurities such as urine and excrement.[5]

The ascetic's relation to the wider community may eventually be marked by an even more off-balance and "mad" way of life which is more conducive to his spiritual progress: he should wear no religious marks which connect him with any sect at all; he should engage in offensive practices such as snoring, etc., to turn away the curious; he should welcome insults from people who judge him inferior; he should wander about, vulnerable to the assaults of unfriendly people; he should behave like a ghoul, dirty, covered with ashes, acting strange; he should pretend to sleep even when he is awake; he should tremble like an arthritic man; he should walk with a limp; he should dally with women; he should speak nonsense. In these and other ways he will offend the righteous and merit their abuse; he will learn the way of penance and all his sins will be destroyed. In the end, he will be abandoned by everyone, left alone to think only of Shiva, the terrible God who is his only protector.[6]

While we may not imagine ourselves living in such odd ways, Shiva, mad saints, and peripheral communities have something important to teach us. They remind us, first of all, that God can be odd, alien, unfamiliar, shocking, and scandalous; the experience of God makes at least some people peculiar; being in contact with God and God's holy people can be a very unsettling affair. Authentic encounters with God do not always contribute to social harmony, and living a respected religious life may not be the best preparation for actually encountering God.

Even in our own traditions, we ought not reduce God to a familiar figure, for then we may lose God, mistaking a comfortable image for the living presence. All the more so when we explore other traditions. If we are not open to encountering God in unexpected and disturbing ways that do not fit our experience thus far, the exploration will have little vitality and little value. There is no reason to expect that our encounter with the Hindu religious tra-

---

5. As stated in chap. 1 of the *Pasupata Sutram.*
6. As stated in chap. 3 of the *Pasupata Sutram.*

ditions will be only pleasing, uplifting, and comforting. Being shocked can be a sign that the new wisdom is getting through to us.

Sometimes, however, what we encounter may be something unexpected according to our established categories. With time, however, we may begin to understand and appreciate it. For example, we can be put off by the fact of so many gods and goddesses, by the many names, by the bewildering imagery, the colors and shapes, the extra heads and arms and legs, the many weapons these deities hold. After some time, we may adjust our categories and appreciate these new presentations of the divine.

Sometimes, however, things upset us because we do understand them and still do not like them. We may choose to keep disagreeing with some of what we see, even after we understand it. We may simply disapprove of ascetical and ritual systems out of touch with the real world; we may disapprove of hierarchical inequalities and the relegation of women to a second-class status; we may reject obsessive concentrations of power. To decide in advance to approve of everything that is new is no better than disliking everything new.

But learning the religious ways of other traditions may sometimes entail real danger, real loss. We need to be careful when we go forth to a new spiritual place. Exploring a religious tradition other than our own can be so deeply unsettling that our faith becomes unhinged. In the beginning we may just want to enrich our faith, but in the end we may lose hold of our tradition and familiar way of living. Sometimes this is a good experience too, but some people will be hurt if they venture too far from what is familiar to them; e.g., the young or the naive may step blindly into situations and experiences for which they are not prepared. Though fear of unfamiliar religious sects and cults is usually unjustified, sometimes it is right to fear that something may go wrong.

On the whole, though, there is no way forward religiously other than to take new and unexpected encounters seriously, to follow through on them, facing up to strange forms of God and strange ways of being religious. If we cut ourselves off from other religious traditions, that too may diminish and sap our religious vitality. Like the sages in the forest, we may become too comfortable even in our piety and recoil from the stranger who marks a new arrival of God in our lives; we may curse the stranger and make ourselves sterile.

In all cases basic rules apply: be disposed to respect other religions as you respect your own; do not reduce a tradition to what you dislike about it: "First take the log out of your own eye, and then you will see clearly to take the speck out of your neighbor's eye" (Matt. 7:5).

ACT TWO: SURRENDERING TO MYSTERY

After so lengthy a reflection on the value of religious madness and differ-ence, let us return to our drama. "Act Two" — entitled perhaps "Surrendering to Mystery" — picks up during the crisis that ensues after Shiva's lingam has fallen off and the whole world gone cold and dark. The sages are confused and forlorn, for their virtue too has fallen; they can achieve nothing. They seek advice from Brahma, a senior and very wise god, often charged with the task of making the world. Though Brahma is very much less a universal reality than Brahman, which the *Crest Jewel* identifies as the central mystery of the universe, he is a very well placed deity, and he can always figure out what is going on, how one thing leads to another. But even he does not im-mediately know the answer to their questions about the naked intruder. After deep meditation, though, he realizes who their visitor was, and he explains to the sages that it was Shiva, the great Lord of all, the true creator and protector and destroyer of the universe. Shiva, he tells them, is the supreme master of the asceticism they have been earnestly attempting. Brahma ad-vises them to return home and make their peace with Shiva, for there is no alternative.

The sages go home and worship Shiva for a year. Interestingly, this pe-riod is also the coming of springtime. Cold and death give way to warmth and new life, and the sages themselves begin to come back to life. Through-out this springtime the sages worship Shiva's lingam, now a pillar which represents him as present though without imaginable form. Even today the lingam is one of the most popular representations of Shiva, and one finds small and large lingams in every Shiva temple. The lingam is a union of opposites; it is a physical presence of the invisible God who is yet without form. Just before the myth we are considering there is another myth in the preceding chapter of the *Brahmanda Purana* about how Brahma along with Vishnu — here not the lord of the universe we encountered in chapter 4 — discovered the lingam and instituted worship of it. Vishnu recounts what he and Brahma found:

We stood there with palms joined in reverence before the splendor and power of the luster of Shiva. We saw the mass of splendor increasing in size. It was excessively wonderful. Brahma and I hastily rushed to-ward that massive flame, which rose up piercing heaven and earth. In the midst of that massive splendor, we saw an exceedingly resplendent lingam of the size of one span; it was not manifest, yet it was radiant. That lingam was neither of gold nor silver nor rock; it could not be specified, we could not even contemplate it. It was visible, yet invisible. It was richly endowed with thousands of sparks. It was wondrous and mysterious; it was endowed with great refulgence, and it was increasing in size, tremendously. Bursts of flame spread everywhere. It was frightful to all living beings. It was extremely terrible in its features. It appeared to pierce heaven and earth.[7]

Vishnu and Brahma try to find the top and bottom of the lingam, but they cannot, for the lingam is infinite, beyond even their reach. Even these great gods surrender to Shiva and worship him in the lingam, the form of his unimaginable greatness.

In the minds of most ordinary Hindus, the lingam is not the phallus of Shiva nor even a phallic symbol; it is simply the universal symbol of Shiva's transcendence and mystery. We must respect this common viewpoint, but after reading the myth it is hard to avoid attributing some phallic significance to the lingam. A tall, thin column, it seems to signify both Shiva's sexual power and also the unshaken self-control of this master who neither represses nor surrenders to desire. The lingam usually stands inside a yoni, the circular form which represents the female organ, so worshiping the lingam is to approach the male together with the female, Shiva with his wife, Uma.

To worship the lingam is to praise Shiva as the highest Lord of the universe and to surrender to that mystery. By accepting the lingam as the sign of Shiva, the sages find a new foundation for their religious practice. As they undertake this worship, they affirm the paradoxical nature of Shiva, who had previously frightened and annoyed them; they step beyond the secure and entirely predictable asceticism of their past.

After the sages have worshiped the lingam for a year, Shiva returns just as he had come in the first place. They praise him without reserve: "You are the source and vitality of all, the Lord who carries the trident, the Lord who rides the bull, the Lord of demons, the God in all the Scriptures, the One by whose power everyone who does anything does it, the Master of amazing power."[8]

They ask Shiva to show himself as before — in his naked form, with his lingam restored. What they had rejected, now they accept positively, without compromise. In grand words that recall the praise of Krishna in the *Bhagavad Gita,* the sages praise Shiva:

---

7. *Brahmanda Purana* 1.2.26.19–24; as translated by Tagare, 260–61, with slight adaptations.
8. Here and in the following paragraph I have paraphrased their hymns.

You are the naked one with bells, hideous and frightening yet also the golden one; you are the foul-smelling and the sweet-smelling, the one who wears ashes from the cremation ground; you dwell in forests, you wear a snake for your sacred thread; you are the Lord of whom everything is a part, the one who makes everything; among mountains, you are the tallest, Meru; among animals, you are the greatest, the bull; among the Vedas, you are the supreme sound, OM, from which all sound comes; you are the great destroyer, the Lord of fire, the Lord of immortality, the Lord beyond limits, the naked Lord who is male and female; you are the Lord of theory and practice, all that we think and all that we do.

With these words they have accepted and internalized the contradictions which previously had shocked them, and they are finally in a position to learn from their God. So they conclude by asking Shiva to teach them.

Willingness to be taught is a religious virtue. As we have already seen, this willingness is the reason the student in the *Crest Jewel* could truly learn from his teacher, why Arjuna could learn from Krishna; Sacchaka's confidence that he knew everything was one reason why he had such a hard time learning from the Buddha. We need to surrender unconditionally before God, with our minds opened, if we are to acquire religious wisdom. Like the sages, we may also have to confess our limitations and seek the help of someone wiser than ourselves, a spiritual guide like Brahma who knows how things work. As we learn, we need also to be patient, for learning comes to fruition only gradually, as gently and slowly as the arrival of springtime in a cold climate. If we are studying Indian wisdom, we should really want to learn, and we should be willing to be taught. Like the sages, at first we may be put off and may have to learn to imagine God differently.

We may also have to reconsider the signs, symbols, and sacraments which have provided the concrete form of our prayer lives, making an account of the things we do and things we keep around us to remind us of God. A Christian might first of all return for a new look at the symbol of the crucified Jesus. Like the lingam, the crucifix puts before the believer the unadorned, shocking mystery of God in our midst. St. Paul reminds us that the cross is a stumbling block which trips up the powerful and learned:

For the message about the cross is foolishness to those who are perishing, but to us who are being saved it is the power of God. For it is written, "I will destroy the wisdom of the wise, and the discernment of the discerning I will thwart" [Isa. 29:14]. Where is the one who is wise? Where is the debater of this age? Has not God made foolish the wisdom of the world? For since, in the wisdom of God, the world did not know God through wisdom, God decided, through the foolishness of our proclamation, to save those who believe.... For God's foolishness is wiser than human wisdom, and God's weakness is stronger than human strength. (1 Cor. 1:18–21, 25)

Though it is important to recognize and maintain our roots, it is also important not to cling to an entirely settled wisdom. We need to be people who can still be surprised by God. If we want to reaffirm our traditional images and yet also welcome God in ways that reach beyond what we have known thus far, we may have to put together new and more complex images which can help us to contemplate the spiritual meaning of religious pluralism; we may need to bring together the familiar and the unfamiliar in order to contemplate them in one place, at one moment. For instance, one could place the crucifix and the lingam together, these two great stumbling blocks believers must confront if they are to encounter God directly, in truth. The crucifix and the lingam are not the same, by any means, but each breaks down the confidence and self-assuredness by which believers inoculate themselves against God. If we contemplate them together, each is renewed by the other, and each can push us more vigorously to accept humbly and openly the wisdom that intrudes upon us in today's changing world.

ACT THREE: MOST HOLY NAKEDNESS

"Act Three" — entitled perhaps "Most Holy Nakedness" — is given over to Shiva's teaching. The sages ask Shiva to explain what they had seen:

The great Lord was pleased, and he came and spoke to the sages: "I am pleased with your asceticism, for you have kept your vows well. Ask for anything you want...." They all bowed to the great God and said, "Tell us about bathing with ashes, nakedness, the 'left-handedness' that goes against acceptable standards, and about what is to be used and what is not to be used — Lord, we wish to know all of this."

Three points are basic to Shiva's teaching: the wearing of ash, as the reconciliation of opposites; nakedness, as the way of openness; union with Shiva, as the ultimate goal. Let us consider each in turn.

Holy Ash

First, there is the matter of ash:

I will proclaim this entire matter to you this very day. I am Fire joined with Soma [the intoxicating liquid of life], I am Soma mingled with Fire.... The supreme purification of this entire universe is to be accomplished by my ashes, for I place my seed in ashes and sprinkle creatures with it. One who has done everything which must be done by fire will master the past, present, and future. By means of my ashes, by my seed, you will be released from all sins.... For I am the entire universe: everything, moving and still, has Fire and Soma for its soul. I am Fire of great energy, my wife Ambika is Soma. I am both Fire and Soma, I myself am the Male joined with Nature herself.... Henceforth, ashes will be used for protection against inauspicious people, and in houses where women give birth. One who has purified his soul by bathing in ashes, conquering anger and subduing the senses, will come into my presence, never to be born again....

In India we can still see ascetics wearing ashes but little else. Ash is hygienic, it is simple, it is a sign of asceticism, a mark of the outsider. But ash also signifies the annihilation of desire, its reduction to ashes, the overcoming of oppositions through a new purity and simplicity. Ash reunites Fire and Soma and thus symbolizes the union of male and female too. To wear Shiva's ash is to clothe oneself with his all-encompassing mystery.

It is surely valuable for us too to overcome opposites by encountering and appropriating them, allowing them to unsettle and transform our personal experience. As we experiment with Hindu wisdom, we are challenged to reflect on desire and power, on the ethical and spiritual boundaries that shift as unfamiliar images of the divine disturb and even overwhelm our prior expectations about God. If we persevere in such encounters the result will be something like the production of holy ash. This will be good for our spiritual health; we will become simple, disciplined, detached from the unthinking flow of daily life. Ash touches the body everywhere, but it does not conceal it. We are affected by Hindu wisdom and make it ours, in our own distinctive way; we remain ourselves, even if Hindu wisdom touches us everywhere. To speak of wearing Shiva's ash is to affirm that we are better off in incorporating what is different and disturbing than in fleeing from it.

Naked before God

Shiva next teaches the true meaning of the nakedness which had shocked the sages at the beginning of the myth:

> This creation was created by me, and has shame, delusion, and fear as its soul. The gods and the wise are both born naked, indeed all people are born naked. People with unconquered senses remain naked even if they are clothed in silk: if you are surrounded by unconquered senses, no garment can hide you. Patience, forbearance, noninjury, passionlessness, indifference to honor or dishonor: these alone are the best garments!

Nakedness is a state of soul, not body; it is simplicity of heart. True purity is marked not by what you wear, but by who you are inside. The sages had become angry at Shiva's nakedness because he provoked them to uncover the desires still lurking in their respectable hearts. We have surely heard versions of this wisdom in other places: "You clean the outside of the cup and the plate, but inside they are full of greed and self-indulgence.... First clean the inside of the cup, so that the outside also may become clean" (Matt. 23:25–26).

All this matters when we try to learn from another religious tradition. If we are not already simple and open in our daily lives and within our own traditions, how can we be open when we encounter what is really different? Nakedness marks a willingness to go forward openly and honestly in our study of Hindu wisdom, without protective cover. Naked, uncovered inside and outside, we learn to keep learning, and not to insulate ourselves from the new things God may say and do for us. Rabindranath Tagore, the famous Bengali writer who won the Nobel Prize for Literature in 1912 for his collection entitled *Gitanjali,* expressed in memorable words the vulnerability we must have if we are to keep learning from the God who keeps on giving:

> Thou hast made me endless, such is thy pleasure. This frail vessel thou emptiest again and again, and fillest it ever with fresh life. This little flute of a reed thou hast carried over hills and dales, and hast breathed through it melodies eternally new. At the immortal touch of thy hands my little heart loses its limits in joy and gives birth to utterance ineffable. Thy infinite gifts come to me only on these very small hands of mine. Ages pass, and still thou pourest, and still there is room to fill.[9]

As the Gospel says, "Unless you become like little children, you will never enter the kingdom of God" (Matt. 18:3).

---

9. *Gitanjali, Song Offerings* (New York: Macmillan, 1916), 1.

Totally One

Shiva's third lesson shows that unity with Shiva himself is where the mystery concludes:

> Smear your body until it is pale with my ashes and meditate on me in your heart; and even if you do a thousand things that one ought not do, by bathing in ashes you will cause it all to be burnt to ashes, as fire burns a forest with its energy. If you make a great effort to bathe with ashes three times a day, you will become a leader among my people; if you become holy by merging yourself with me, you will obtain the supreme elixir of life and become completely free.

As we have seen, to put on ash signifies purity, the desire to have no cover but Shiva alone: ash on the body, Shiva in the heart. In turn, dependence on him yields power and leadership, and complete freedom.

Near the end of the *Pashupata Sutram,* wearing ash comes to signify the process of ever more intimate identification with Shiva. You become free, no longer entangled by what you do or fail to do; you repeat your special mantra and live alone in a cremation ground; you live in poverty, without asking for anything; you reach intimate union with Shiva, remembering him always, your mind fixed upon his grace alone. Then you will be all alone, free, fearless, without sorrow. In the end, there will be nothing but Shiva: "May Shiva be mine, always, simply Shiva," nothing but Shiva, God who visits us from beyond the reaches of our minds, God who draws us beyond every protective covering into God's own mystery.[10]

TO DWELL IN MYSTERY

The encounter of Shiva with the sages in the pine forest is memorable even as a story, yet it is rich in deeper meanings; the reader is invited to become part of the story and to surrender to Shiva. That he is the Lord of mystery is often reexpressed in even simpler mystical terms. This poem by Manikkavachakar, a South Indian saint, captures the essence of encountering Shiva:

> Great river of exceeding tenderness, flowing without end,
> Ambrosia I can never have enough of, my Lord without limits,
> Light hidden in the hearts of those who do not seek you,

---

10. As stated near the end of chap. 4 of the *Pasupata Sutram.*

you melt me into water, you stand within me as my dear life.
You are without pleasure and pain, yet within both;
you are loving to those who love, you are in everything, yet not there;
you are the light that shines in deep darkness, great and unmanifest;
you are the beginning, end, middle, yet none of these.
You can be known by the wise in their minds but still
you elude every eye, you are known only by the subtlest awareness.
You never go, you never come, you never mingle, holy one,
guardian protector, dazzling light which eyes cannot see, flood of
    delight,
you are a father to me, yet more than that, ever shining, a subtle
    realization beyond words,
in this ever-changing world with all its various forms you are knowl-
    edge itself.[11]

Encountering Shiva becomes something deeper and gentler as its mystery is disclosed in poetry. The surprise is no longer that of a naked man scream- ing and dancing, but rather of a light which is too bright for eyes used to shadows, a presence too close to be scrutinized from a safe distance. God is always more than we imagine, perhaps even contrary to our expectations, and yet we must be ready, open: "Blessed are the pure in heart, for they shall see God" (Matt. 5:8).

I remember once visiting the large and ancient temple of Shiva in Chi- dambaram, South India. I walked through the circling pathways within the temple, finally reaching the central inner shrine. There, within the holiest shrine, is a final interior space, seemingly totally dark. But it is there that the lingam of Shiva is said ultimately to rest. When I looked in, I saw only an empty space. My guide suggested that the lingam was there but I did not yet have eyes to see it.

Even if we do not interpret our encounter with India as an encounter with Shiva, shocking or mysterious or gracious, encountering God still demands a radical openness to whatever God may want to be for us. For a time, we may feel that we have lost and not gained, that we have no protection, no covering. But like the sages in the pine forest, we must eventually surrender to this mystery, night brighter than the day, if we are to find the one we have always been seeking. There is no alternative.

---

11. Verses 66–82 from the opening song, "Siva Puranam," of the *Tiruvacakam* of Manikkavachakar; from the translation of G. U. Pope, *The Tiruvacagam* (Madras: University of Madras, 1979), with slight adaptations.

6

Mother of the Universe

Krishna, the celestial Lord come down among humans, the unimaginably beautiful face upon which you might gaze forever without growing tired; Shiva, the God who can be contrary, paradoxical, a mystery to whom you must surrender yourself again and again: these are two powerful visions of God that Hindus urge upon us, and they give us enough to reflect upon for a very long time. But the Hindu tradition tells us that God is still more, for God is also our Mother, the source of all life. Every experience, every sight and sound and taste and touch and smell, brings us near to the great Goddess. To understand Hindu wisdom more completely, we must therefore also think about goddesses.

I first thought about Hindu goddesses in the 1970s when I was teaching in Kathmandu, Nepal. During a school holiday I went on a field trip with a Jesuit anthropologist. In a small village in the lower ranges of the Himalayas, we came upon the beginning of a local festival. It was intriguing, so we changed our plans and stayed there for several days, just to watch. At the center of the festival was the sacrifice of a young buffalo; this was done right in front of the Goddess shrine, since killing the buffalo commemorated how the Goddess once killed the mighty buffalo demon. In the course of the rite two men who had entered trance states drank blood right from the buffalo three times, dancing around the animal and in front of the Goddess. Some said that this drinking, vivid though it was, was just symbolic of the triumph of good over evil; as the buffalo is killed and the blood consumed, so the Goddess destroys evil and takes up our burdens. Others said that the meaning was more literal: the Goddess was angry and through the men was actually drinking the blood offered to her. Either way, it was an unforgettable ritual to observe.

Over time I read more about goddesses. I learned that there has been a long tradition of honoring the Goddess — Devi, Durga, Kali — as the ultimate destroyer of all evil. For millennia, though, goddesses seem to have been marginalized in written traditions, and some communities remained almost entirely silent about them, despite the fact that the cult of goddesses seems to have been always popular among a wide range of people. Eventually they made their presence felt in the mainstream traditions, even in the major orthodox communities. In preceding chapters, we have already met some of these goddesses. In chapter 1, we saw how the original person became female and male in the course of the creative act, and how they interacted, the male Fire with the female Soma. In chapter 4, Krishna danced with the cowherd women, and related especially to Radha, the cowherd woman who was recognized as his eternal consort come down to earth with him. Likewise, though in a different way, Andal was revered as a true eternal consort of Krishna, the Earth Goddess. In chapter 5, when Shiva danced in the forest, Uma (Parvati) was there dancing with him, for they can never be apart. One could spend a great deal of time tracing the relationship between the male and female in Hinduism and charting ways in which goddesses have been presented.

KILLING THE BUFFALO DEMON

I learned too of the vivid myths which emphasize the power of the Goddess, like the myth behind the animal sacrifice I had witnessed. According to the most famous version of her origins and divine deeds, there was a time when the world was in unprecedented crisis because it was tormented by a great male demon; even working together, the gods were unable to subdue him. Although the Goddess was not involved in the struggle and was off meditating by herself, in desperation the gods approached her and begged her to destroy the demon for them. They gave her all their weapons and the combined force of their powers. Riding her lion, she goes forth to meet the demon, taunting him and provoking him into a battle he must ultimately lose — thereby reversing the creation myth we saw in chapter 2, for now it is the woman who pursues the man:

> When the fierce Goddess saw the great demon attacking, swollen with anger, she became frantic to slay him. She hurled her noose over him and bound the great demon. But when he was thus bound in the great struggle he abandoned his buffalo form and became a lion. When the Mother cut off his head, he appeared as a man with a sword in his hand and a shield made of hide, but the Goddess took her arrows and quickly pierced the man. Then he became a great elephant, who pulled

at her great lion with his trunk and trumpeted, but the Goddess took her sword and cut off his trunk as he pulled. Then the great demon once more assumed his buffalo shape and shook the triple world, moving and still. Enraged by this, the furious mother of the universe drank the supreme wine again and again; her eyes became red, and she laughed. . . . The Goddess said, "Roar and roar for a moment, you fool, while I drink this sweet wine. The gods will soon roar when I have slain you here." Then she leaped up and mounted that great demon and kicked him in the neck with her foot and pierced him with her trident. When he was struck by her foot he came half way out of his own mouth, for he was enveloped by the Goddess's heroic power. As the demon came half way out, fighting, the Goddess cut off his head with her great sword, and he fell.[1]

The Goddess is revered as the protector of the good, destroyer of evil. People still recount her deeds and praise her in songs and images, in rituals such as I saw in the village.

Despite the violent power often connected with her story, however, the Goddess is also the great Mother, the source and protector of every being. Life comes from the Goddess, and every experience is an experience of her. Even death is simply her final gift, for it too is part of life. Ramprasad, an eighteenth-century Bengali poet-saint, addressed the Goddess as his own Mother. He had a vivid sense of her enormous power and universal presence:

O Mother, You are present in every form;
You are in the entire universe and in its tiniest and most trifling things.
Wherever I go and wherever I look,
I see you, O Mother, present in your cosmic form.
The whole world — earth, fire, water, air —
All are your forms, Mother, the whole world of birth and death.
"Mountains, plants, animals living on land and in the water,
All moving and unmoving beings in this beautiful world are full of
    Divine will," says Prasad.[2]

Yet even when he called her Mother — the dark Kali, the bright Tara — he retained a strong sense of how terrifying a figure she could be:

---

1. The myth is found in the *Markandeya Purana,* 80; I have used the translation of O'Flaherty in *Hindu Myths,* 248–49, with slight adaptations.
2. As cited by David Kinsley in *The Sword and the Flute* (Santa Barbara: University of California Press, 1975), 116, with slight adaptations.

I am lying at your feet, O Mother, but you do not look at me even once.
You are engrossed in your play, O Kali, you are immersed in thought.
What game do you play on earth, in heaven and hell?

All close their eyes in terror and cry, "Mother! Mother!" grasping your
feet.
O Mother! you have great dissolution in your hand;
Shiva lies at Your feet, absorbed in bliss;
You laugh aloud, striking terror; streams of blood flow from your
limbs.

O Tara, doer of good, the good of all, grantor of safety, O Mother, grant
me safety.
Mother Kali, take me in your arms, Mother Kali, take me in your arms!
Mother, come now as the Goddess Tara with a smiling face and clad in
white,
as dawn descends on dense darkness of night.
Mother, terrifying Kali, I have worshiped you alone for so long,
My worship is finished now, O Mother, bring down your sword![3]

Only by total surrender can a person take shelter with her.

The whole topic of goddesses is of course very interesting and timely.
Most of us belong to religious traditions which have no place for goddesses,
and even the mention of goddesses provokes strong reactions in some circles.
Sometimes we do find a place for feminine elements in our piety: e.g., Jews
and Christians reverence Divine Wisdom; Christians and Muslims honor the
Virgin Mary. But many are still not comfortable in attributing female features
and names to God, especially if this would mean "God" is also "Goddess."
Even when we try not to think of God as just male, many will opt instead for
a God who is beyond gender, avoiding the idea that God can be conceived
of as female. Indeed, some people seem more comfortable with atheism than
with goddesses.

Nonetheless, if we are serious about seeking wisdom and seriously want
to learn from India, we must not be put off by these factors. The Goddess tradition is too important to ignore and, as we shall see, too valuable to bypass.
If we do not reflect on Hindu goddesses, we will not have learned enough
from Hindu wisdom.

Out of the many approaches one might take to the study of goddesses, in
this chapter I focus on just one text about a Goddess, the *Saundarya Lahari,*

---

3. As cited by Kinsley in *The Sword and the Flute,* 119–20, with slight adaptations.

i.e., the *Ocean of Beauty*. This text, composed in Sanskrit verses, is perhaps one thousand years old or more. Unlike texts we have dealt with in previous chapters, the *Ocean of Beauty* is not a narrative, nor is it dramatic in any ordinary sense. Neither is it abstract. It is rather a very vivid and theologically advanced presentation and visualization of the Goddess and how to approach her properly. The *Ocean of Beauty* is 103 verses long and is divided into two sections. The 41 verses of Part One proclaim the true nature and greatness of the Goddess. The 62 verses of Part Two visualize her from head to toe. As we shall see by looking at the commonly available Sastri and Ayyangar edition which I have used throughout, the *Ocean of Beauty* is a book accompanied by a rich tradition of practices meant to enhance the realization of its wisdom.[4]

In the following sections we will examine the *Ocean of Beauty* from six vantage points, as follows. First, the worshiper proclaims the Goddess to be present everywhere, in world and self; this is the major point in Part One. Second, the worshiper finds her present everywhere and in everything; this is explained in relation to the seven chakras, i.e., the seven physical and psychological points of energy encoded in the human self, the universe, and the Goddess herself. Third, the worshiper contemplates the Goddess from head to toe, enjoying her beauty in each aspect; this is the major point in Part Two. Fourth, the worshiper must learn from a teacher the proper way to worship and realize the Goddess. Fifth, the worshiper realizes the Goddess more fully by stimulating his or her sense awareness to the maximum, learning to hear, to see, and to act in a truly awakened fashion. Sixth, even the worshiper can point the way to deeper religious understanding, as we learn from the nineteenth-century saint Ramakrishna, whose Goddess experience shows us how to understand the diversity of religions deeply and religiously.

FINDING THE GODDESS EVERYWHERE, IN WORLD AND SELF

Part One of the *Ocean of Beauty* praises the Goddess by a careful and loving recollection of who she is and what she means to her worshipers. Though she is described in detail, the account is almost entirely devoid of mythological references; it is both more personal and more philosophical, for she always exists now, in this place. The following are some examples of how she is presented. Although the Goddess is always with Lord Shiva, she

---

4. All translations of the *Saundarya Lahari* (*The Ocean of Beauty*) are taken, with slight adaptations, from the edition and translation by S. S. Sastri and T. R. Srinivasa Ayyangar, *Saundarya Lahari* (*The Ocean of Beauty*) (Madras and Wheaton, Ill.: Theosophical Publishing House, 1992). Diagrams and other information on this text are also drawn from this edition.

remains independent. She is his spouse, his body, half of him. She belongs to him as his power, but this means that he can be powerful because he is with her; even Vishnu (Hari), Shiva (Hara), Brahma (Virincha), and the other gods praise her:

> Only if he is joined with you, his power, can Shiva rule.
> Without you he cannot even move.
> So how dare I, so lacking in merit, salute or praise you
> who are worthy of the adoration of Hari, Hara, Virincha, and all the
>   others? (v. 1)

So too, like him, she is the destroyer of evil and vanquisher of demons.

She is a lovely and generous woman. She is the daughter of the snow-capped mountain, red like the dawn, radiant as the morning sunlight, sweet as honey, a protector and place of refuge, the bestower of prosperity. She is the Mother of all. So too, she is wisdom and speech, the flood of consciousness and bliss, the Goddess of all learning. All greatness is encoded in her secret name. She is the source of all words, yet her eternal glory reaches beyond words; even the scriptures lie prostrate at her feet. Indeed, she is everything in nature, external realities and their inner meaning:

> You are Mind, you are Ether, you are Wind, as Fire you ride the Wind, you are Water, you are Earth. As you transform yourself, there is nothing beyond you. To transform your self into every form, you have consciousness and bliss as your form and way of being, O consort of Shiva! (v. 35)

Likewise, she is the creator and destroyer of everything; just by opening or closing her eyes, she creates or destroys the world:

> Daughter of the mountain king, the wise say that the world dissolves and is created as you close and open your eyes; to save the world from dissolution, you never close your eyes! (v. 55)

The Goddess is worshiped by the gods. She wears the crowns of Indra, Vishnu, and Brahma, who are always at her feet, as this verse charmingly reminds us:

> Glory to the words of your servants! When all at once you rush to greet Shiva, who has come to your abode, please be careful: avoid the

crown of Brahma before you! Beware, you might trip over the hard
crest of Krishna, slayer of Kairabha! Please, don't step on the headgear
of Indra, foe of Jambha. All three lie prostrate before you. (v. 29)

The worshiper must submit to the Goddess, completely and with total
devotion. Every aspect of daily life takes on new meaning in relation to her:

Whatever action I take is for your worship; my foolish words are the
whispering of your prayer; the deeds of my hands are gestures em-
ployed in your worship; my wandering steps circle you clockwise;
when I eat, it is an offering to you; when I lie down it is a prostration
before you; in every comfort I dedicate my entire self to you. (v. 27)

As worshipers grow in awareness of the Goddess, gradually they come to see
that all reality, everything outside as well as inside the worshiper, is pervaded
with her divine presence.

These points give us at least a sense of how very comprehensively the
Goddess is understood in the *Ocean of Beauty.* But to make this understand-
ing of the Goddess both more concrete and more universal, the *Ocean of
Beauty* teaches the unusual but very important doctrine of the seven chakras.

SEVEN CENTERS OF GODDESS POWER

The chakras are seven "centers" of energy within a person. They are traditionally understood to be located at specific places, the anus, genitals, navel,
heart, throat, forehead, and the crown of the head. While they have physical
positions, they are not simply bodily functions; they are also psychological
and spiritual. While they have psychological and spiritual significance, they
also retain some physical meaning too. These are the seven: the "Foundation Chakra" (*Muladhara*) at the anus; the "Home Chakra" (*Svadhisthana*)
at the genitals; the "Jeweled City" Chakra (*Manipura*) at the navel; the
"Unstruck" Chakra (*Anahata*) at the heart; the "Purifying" Chakra (*Vishud-
dhi*) at the throat; the "Commanding" Chakra (*Ajna*) at the brow; and the
"Thousand-Petal" Chakra (*Sahasrara*) at the crown of the head. The chakras
are traditionally understood to be located within the worshiper, yet also
within the Goddess herself.[5] She rises up through all seven of them piercing
and filling them; she travels up through them and down again:

---

5. The *Ocean of Beauty* does not say that the Goddess moves within the chakras of the human
body as distinct from her own body, possibly because this very devotional text sees everything in
the Goddess herself. The parallel between the chakras in her body and the chakras in the human
body has been assumed by most traditional readers, and I too will assume it in what follows.

You pierce Earth in the Foundation Chakra, Water in the Jeweled City Chakra, Fire in the Home Chakra, Wind in the heart's Unstruck Chakra, Air in the Purifying Chakra above that (at the throat), Mind in the Commanding Chakra between the brows. In that way you pierce the entire holy path and take pleasure with your Lord in the secrecy of the Thousand-Petal Chakra;

you fill that holy path of nerves with a stream of nectar that flows from beneath your feet; then, as a serpent of three and a half coils, you descend to your place in the resplendent lunar regions, you sleep again in the cave deep within the Foundation Chakra. (vv. 9–10)

The chakras are also connected with the constituent elements of the universe; the general parallelism among the elements, the chakras, and the body — divine and human — can be summarized in this way:

Cosmic Element	Name of Chakra	Physical Location
earth	Foundation (*Muladhara*)	anus
fire	Home (*Svadhisthana*)	genitals
water	Jeweled City (*Manipura*)	navel
wind	Unstruck (*Anahata*)	heart
air	Purifying (*Vishuddhi*)	throat
mind	Commanding (*Ajna*)	brow
consciousness	Thousand-Petal (*Sahasrara*)	top of head

The Goddess pervades every element, and the worshiper must recognize her presence on all seven cosmic and personal levels:

You are Mind, you are Air, you are Wind, you ride the Wind as Fire, you are Water, you are Earth. As you transform yourself, there is nothing beyond you. To transform yourself into every form, you assume the form of Consciousness and Bliss, O Consort of Shiva! (v. 35)

The worshiper is supposed to meditate on each chakra and visualize the Goddess as standing there in a specific form, along with Shiva, and so to begin to realize the energy of that chakra.

In modern manuals, the verses which guide the realization of the chakras are often accompanied by helpful colored charts; but even by themselves the verses stimulate and stretch the mind. I suggest that the reader spend some time with each of the following key verses. Study them, leave aside what seems too mysterious or obscure, imagine them as you are able, and see what meanings and images come to you:

I salute the supreme Benevolent Lord who abides in your Commanding Chakra (at the brow), who shines with the radiance of countless suns and moons. You are the Supreme Consciousness nestled by his side. By worshiping you both with devotion, we begin to live in the region of light beyond the reach of sun and moon and fire too, a place no sorrow can touch.

I worship Shiva in your Purifying Chakra (at the throat), as clear as pure crystal, source for Air itself. I worship you, Goddess, for only with you can Shiva act. Radiant, like moonbeams, you share one form, banishing from the universe its inner darkness, so it dances with joy like the partridge!

You are a pair of swans who care only for the honey of Wisdom in the lotus that blooms in the Unstruck Chakra (at the heart), as you glide across that Lake of Mind where the wise reside. I worship you! Your cry echoes in the teachings of all eighteen schools of learning, you extract the good from the bad, like milk from water.

Mother, I glorify the Lord who dissolves everything, who abides in your Home Chakra (at the genitals); with you he presides over Fire, but you are the great Goddess who brings things into harmony again. Your glance rains pity, cooling the world burnt by his furious, raging stare.[6]

I reverence the dark-blue cloud that dwells forever in your Jeweled City Chakra (at the navel); it is the energy of lightning, the luster that conquers all darkness, a rainbow of gems sparkling among jewels, rain showered upon all three worlds scorched by fire and sun. (vv. 36–40)

Even Shiva's famous cosmic dance is visualized in relation to the Goddess's own dance:

In your Foundation Chakra (at the anus) I contemplate Shiva who dances wildly in all nine moods, and I contemplate you as the nine-fold self, the Goddess who brings things into harmony again. I am intent upon your own amorous dance. I mark the passing of creation by you and Shiva. I confess that this world is ruled by you: by your grace you are the world's Mother and Father. (v. 41)

---

6. It is a bit confusing to see that the Home Chakra appears at the genitals in this verse, while the Jeweled City Chakra appears at the navel in the next verse, when we would expect the reverse. Sastri and Ayyangar note the discrepancy and suggest that because Fire is superior to Water in the order of the universe, the Home Chakra, connected with Fire, is given first in this instance.

The Goddess is one with Shiva who is her male principle; she pervades the universe and makes it real. She permeates the worshiper's own self at every level of human being. To worship her is therefore not to worship just one being among many, someone near or far, high or low. Rather, it is to encounter the energy of the entire universe in its breadth and in every detail all at once in the Goddess; it is to see oneself anew in the radiance of the unlimited reality, the Goddess who permeates everything. The *Ocean of Beauty* invites the worshiper not simply to acknowledge such totality as possible or true, but to experience everything all at once, at least for a moment.

CONTEMPLATING THE GODDESS, HEAD TO TOE

The powerful invitation put forward in the first part of the *Ocean of Beauty* is not easily realized. The second part of the text, supported by the additional practices to which we shall refer later, is aimed at turning the ideal into an experienced reality. Part Two offers a lengthy contemplation of the Goddess as she is visualized slowly and carefully from head to toe. Who the Goddess is and how she relates to self and world is gradually realized through this extended meditation on her physical form, each verse lingering in meditative enjoyment on one of her features. The meditation begins with her hair and moves down gradually toward her feet, as these verses illustrate:

Spouse of Shiva, your locks of hair are thick, shining and soft, like a field of blue lilies in bloom: may they drive away all our darkness! Even the flowers on the trees in the garden of Indra, king of the gods, gain their fragrance from your hair. (v. 43)

I contemplate your forehead, shining bright and clear in its radiant beauty, as a second crescent adorning your crown. Merging, these crescents become a full moon anointed with nectar. (v. 46)

Daughter of the mountain king, the wise say that the world dissolves and is created as you close and open your eyes; to save the world from dissolution, you never close your eyes! (v. 55)

Daughter of the mountain, like the milk filling your breasts, the milk ocean fills your heart with poetic verse, it rises up and gives excellence to the very best of human poets. (v. 75)

Daughter of the mountain, may your waist itself grant us safety. It is slim, so narrow it seems to give way at the navel; it is as fragile as a tree standing on the bank of a river. (v. 79)

Your feet give wealth at all times, immediately to those in need. Your toes shake in laughter, they mock the magic wish-filling trees of paradise — which by shaking their branches give only small gifts to the residents of heaven. (v. 89)

The sun itself is a mirror of crystal for your feet; he withdrew his beams for fear of burning your face which is the lotus in his own heart, never troubled by the moon, always in bloom. (v. 94)

Actually, one might have expected the description to move upward toward her head, as a worshiper might experience divine energy rising up through the chakras. But this downward motion seems essential, so that the worshiper finishes in a humble, expectant position at her feet — where every devotee belongs.

At the end of *Ocean of Beauty* the poet praises her in a way that self-consciously takes the poet's own skill into account:

You are my Treasure, ever smiling, possessed of boundless good qualities, skilled in holding the scales in balance, uninterrupted fountain of wisdom, ever abiding in well-controlled minds. You are bound by no social conventions, your feet are glorified by all the scriptures, you are untouched by dangers, eternal One — so bless these words of praise!

Mother of all poetry, I have composed these verses in your honor, but my words come from you; it is like praising the sun with a small flame, the moon with dewdrops, the ocean with a libation of water. (vv. 102–3)

In the course of this careful visualization, the *Ocean of Beauty* does not actually step back and tell the worshiper what to *do* with the verses. It is in many ways a restrained text, largely symbolic, reticent in its demands on the worshiper. There are tantric rites which work through meditation on the Goddess even in a very literal fashion, as a male worshiper worships a young woman installed before him in place of the Goddess. In such rites, her body becomes for him the Goddess's physical presence, and it is upon the young woman that he then meditates head to toe. In a famous example, the nineteenth-century saint Ramakrishna installed his wife, Sarada Devi, in place of the Goddess, and worshiped her as Divine Mother — thereby raising both her and himself into a high state of consciousness.[7] In the *Ocean of Beauty,* by contrast, the worshiper is asked to meditate on the Goddess with the mind's eye, visualizing all her different aspects within the mind and not in any exterior place or person. Yet even this text has been surrounded by practices which the worshiper can undertake to bring home its truth. Before turning to those, though, it is crucial that we first of all take note of a simple but important point.

LEARNING FROM A TEACHER

The *Ocean of Beauty* is clear, but even after careful study it may still seem confusing. I fear my readers too will be perplexed by some of the verses, by the chakras, and by the additional details still to appear in the following pages. Further study of commentaries will surely help, even in the excellent condensed version given by Sastri and Ayyangar, but our confusion will not entirely vanish due to a closer or more scholarly reading. It is probable that neither the text itself, as a book to be read, nor any written commentary added to it, can give sufficient information presented wisely in the right way by which to make perfectly clear how a devotee is to understand and worship the Goddess.

Additional guidance is therefore required from a teacher, a guru. This is true in just about any Hindu tradition, but it seems particularly important here. The serious student must seek out a competent teacher who is part of the living tradition of Goddess wisdom. This teacher will know the tradition and be able to remember, present, and illustrate connections and applications not explicit in the written text itself. Like any good teacher or spiritual counselor, the teacher will know the student and help the student to understand and worship more fruitfully. Without a teacher, the information given amply in the verses of the *Ocean of Beauty* and summarized very briefly in these pages will not fit together properly, and our understanding of the Goddess will remain confused on the details and their implementation too. With this caution in mind, let us continue our initial exploration of Goddess wisdom, by examining three of the supplementary practices which help the devotee to realize the Goddess in sound, sight, and action.

---

7. My reading has given me only a little information about how women worship the Goddess. McDaniel's *The Madness of the Saints,* cited above, is helpful in this regard.

LEARNING TO LISTEN

Realization of the Goddess is filled out first of all through a recovery of pure sound. Each verse is accompanied by a "seed" mantra, a sound such as *hrim, klim, am.* These sounds are first of all meant to be heard, not probed for meanings. For example, let us return to verses 9 and 10, which we saw above:

> You pierce Earth in the Foundation Chakra, Water in the Jeweled City Chakra, Fire in the Home Chakra, Wind in the heart's Unstruck Chakra, Air in the Purifying Chakra above that (at the throat), Mind in the Commanding Chakra between the brows. In that way you pierce the entire holy path and take pleasure with your Lord in the secrecy of the Thousand-Petal Chakra;

> you fill that holy path of nerves with a stream of nectar that flows from beneath your feet; then, as a serpent of three and a half coils, you descend to your place in the resplendent lunar regions, you sleep again in the cave deep within the Foundation Chakra. (vv. 9–10)

According to the Sastri and Ayyangar edition of the *Ocean of Beauty,* these two verses are connected with primal sound in the following way. Verse 9 is connected with the primal sound *yam* repeated three times, followed by *sadhyam* and *am krim.* None of these has any obvious meaning (though *sadhyam* can mean "goal"), and it seems that the sounds are simply to be heard and repeated by the worshiper along with the verse itself. Similarly, verse 10 is to be accompanied by the primal sounds *hrim* and *klim.*

Prior to meditation and careful instruction by a teacher, it is not possible to predict the connection between a particular verse and a particular sound or sounds. The sounds are not drawn from the words in the verses, and there is no obvious meaning common to the verses and the sounds. So the worshiper simply has to recite the verse aloud and utter the sounds along with it — so that the Goddess is *heard* in the purity of the sounds; thus, sound itself becomes a way to meet the Goddess. Primal sounds are connected with almost every verse of the *Ocean of Beauty;* they invite the worshiper to expand the reality of the verses and to experience the interconnection of universe, Goddess, and self through a simple recovery of what it means to hear something.

Ramprasad incorporated primal sounds into his praise of the Goddess. First, he addresses the Goddess as abiding in the chakras:

O Tara, You are in my heart, O Mother, You are the Coiled Serpent Power, You abide in the Foundation Chakra, in the Thousand-Petal Chakra, in the Jeweled City Chakra which is the city of the wish-granting jewel.

Then he envisions her surrounded by the sacred rivers of India, herself curled around Shiva like a snake:

The Ganges River is to the right, the Yamuna River to the left, the Sarasvati River flows through the middle where Shiva and his Female Power abide. In form You are a red serpent, fast asleep, curled around Shiva; to meditate on You is to become blessed.

Finally he introduces primal sounds:

Your form is primal sound. In the Foundation Chakra at the anus, the Home Chakra at the genitals, the Jeweled City Chakra at the navel, the lotuses of the Unstruck Chakra at the heart and Purifying Chakra at the throat, everywhere there are sounds, *va, sa, ra, la, ta, ka, pha,* and *tha;* the sixteen vowels reside in the throat, *ha* and *ksa* between the eyebrows.... So, quickly take Earth, Water, Fire, Wind, [Air, and Mind], and along with them utter the primal sounds *yam, ram, lam, vam, ham,* and *haum!*[8]

I have stressed that the sounds are intended to be heard as simply and purely as possible, without regard to anything else. Thereafter, though, the tantric tradition gives them significance by relating them to the cosmic elements and the chakras. For example, the primal sounds *aim, hrim, srim, aim, klim,* and *sauh* are connected with Earth and with the Foundation Chakra; the primal sounds *ham* and *sah,* to be repeated four times, are connected with Fire and with the Home Chakra.[9] Sometimes primal sounds are connected with primal colors:[10] vowels are said to be white like crystal, *ka* and *ma* are coral blue, *ya* is yellow, *ksa* red.

But still we want to ask, What exactly do *hrim* or *klim* actually mean?

---

8. Excerpted from a song of Ramprasad as translated in *The Cult of Shakti,* J. Sinha (Calcutta, 1981), 133, with slight adaptations.

9. As noted by Sastri and Ayyangar in their summary of traditional commentaries, *Saundarya Lahari,* 77.

10. Sastri and Ayyangar, *Saundarya Lahari,* 88.

Once the priority of the sound itself is appreciated, it would be wrong to insist that the sounds have no meanings whatsoever. Indeed, all kinds of meanings are traditionally assigned. Primal sounds are interpreted as abbreviated forms of words, and these words can be expanded into full mantras:[11] *klim* indicates Memory, and Memory is the son of the God of Love; *hrim* indicates the elemental female symbol (yoni), and she is the Goddess of the Universe; *srim* represents the Goddess Sri, Lakshmi. There are also theories which trace the generation of the pure sounds from one another, all the way back to the original sound, OM.

We should not turn away from these pure sounds as too obscure; nor should we quickly add to them some suitably spiritual meaning. We need to spend time listening to the sounds along with the verses, to repeat them aloud and to hear them, before we think about which meanings they might best have. If we can hear them, they may impress on us that the Goddess is not abstract or distant, that she is as close as sense experience, as every sound we hear. If we do not actually understand *hrim* or *srim,* we might try uttering them slowly, over and over for a period of time, as one might recite a rhythmic prayer. If that is too difficult we might first improve our ability to listen by reciting aloud a favorite poem or listening to a song in a language we do not understand, or just by sitting and listening to the sounds that come in our window.

LEARNING TO SEE

Just as primal sounds enhance the verses of the *Ocean of Beauty,* so too there are visual practices which help the worshiper to see more acutely — the construction and contemplation of designs known as yantras. Yantras are precisely drawn diagrams, sometimes colored, sometimes just lines. They can be imagined as visual mazes which catch and control one's eye, making one focus and gaze more and more attentively. Yantras give the worshiper something to look at while reciting or listening to each verse — not a picture of the Goddess, but an alternate visual experience. Just as one has to learn to hear a pure sound, now one has to learn to look attentively at an intricate or delicately drawn diagram, just to see it, just to let the eye get drawn into it. Because this seeing does not immediately mean anything — there is no recognizable picture to think about, nothing is directly represented — viewing

---

11. Sastri and Ayyangar, *Saundarya Lahari,* 134.

a yantra is a simple action of seeing, and thus an experience of Goddess energy.

By way of example here are the simple yantras for verse 9 (figure 1) and verse 10 (figure 2) with the inscribed pure sounds:

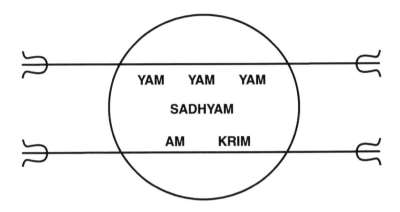

Figure 1. Verse 9.

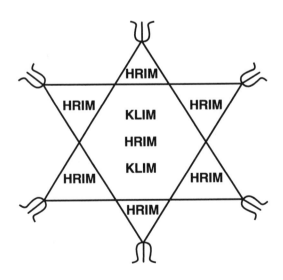

Figure 2. Verse 10.

The most important of all yantras is the Shri Yantra, which is to be visualized along with this verse,

> When I earnestly beseech you with the words, "May I become You!" at that very moment cast your merciful glance on this servant who cries nothing but, "May I become You!" At that very moment, let me be just like you, shining with brilliant crowns worn by gods like Vishnu, Brahma and Indra. (v. 22)

The Shri Yantra is elegant and intriguing (figure 3):

Figure 3. Shri Yantra

The worshiper is expected to draw the yantra, learning to do this properly and exactly; he or she must then sort out, visualize, and internalize all the possible interconnections among the many lines and angles. This too is done along with the recitation of the verses and the hearing of the pure sounds.

Here too we may ask, "What do the yantras mean?" The answer is again the same. As seed mantras are pure sounds which should be heard, yantras are pure visual images simply to be looked at, looked into. The simple act of seeing, experienced as seeing, is a way to experience the Goddess intimately; whenever the worshiper looks at anything, the Goddess is present in that looking. Of course, just as the pure sounds can subsequently take on meanings, the yantras too can be named — as the diagram above is given the name "Shri Yantra" — and even adorned with images of deities and animals.

It will be difficult for most of us to find a teacher from whom to learn the discipline of making and contemplating yantras. We might at least try to see more simply and vividly, by learning to observe things as they are, without superimposing meanings on them. If we can learn just to look at a sunset, or at a piece of nonrepresentational contemporary art, or at the light filtering into a room in the early morning, or even just at a coffee mug sitting on the table, then we will begin to understand what it means to see, and thus to experience the divine energy that makes it possible to see anything at all.

WORSHIPING DAY BY DAY

In addition to contemplating the Goddess from head to toe and practicing pure sounds and yantras, the worshiper can also use the *Ocean of Beauty* ritually. A valuable appendix to Sastri and Ayyangar indicates that traditional commentators and worshipers do not just read the text or meditate on its meaning; they also use it in worship. Each verse can be enacted in set ways, with specific materials, for specific purposes. For example, the ritual directions for verse 22, cited above, indicate that the verse is to be recited daily for forty-five days, one thousand times each day. The yantra accompanying the verse is to be inscribed on a gold plate and worn around the neck. Each day the worshiper makes an offering to the Goddess, of honey, curds (mixed with coconut, sugar, and ghee), milk, and spiced rice. As a result of this faithful practice he or she will achieve worldly desires and have everything a person could need or desire. Other verses, when properly enacted according to similar specifications, lead to other rewards: e.g., release from prison, success in business, mastery over the elements, the safe return of relatives from abroad, virility, female health, the removal of sterility, knowledge of the self. When worshipers of the Goddess say that the *Ocean of Beauty* is a powerful text, they do not mean simply that it contains impressive ideas; when used properly, it is actually effective, it actually enables the worshiper to gain what he or she wants.

We may lack a proper teacher and materials such as gold plates, spiced rice, and the like, and in any case many of us will lack the inclination to observe the rituals connected with the *Ocean of Beauty*. But to appreciate its wisdom we will still do well to observe some ritual more faithfully and attentively as a way of accustoming ourselves anew to the power of ritual. If we are Catholic, for instance, we might try saying the rosary, fifteen decades a day, for a period of thirty days, in front of an image of Mary, the Mother of Jesus, using this prayer over and over:

> Hail Mary, full of grace, the Lord is with you. Blessed are you among women and blessed is the fruit of your womb, Jesus. Holy Mary, Mother of God, pray for us sinners now and at the hour of our death. Amen.

We might address her too in words such as these by the nineteenth-century Jesuit poet Gerard Manley Hopkins:

> Be thou then, O thou dear
> Mother, my atmosphere:
> My happier world, wherein
> To wend and meet no sin;
> Above me, around me lie
> Fronting my forward eye
> With sweet and scarless sky;
> Stir in my ears, speak there
> Of God's love, O live air,
> Of patience, penance, prayer:
> World-mothering air, air wild,
> Wound with thee, in thee isled,
> Fold home, fast fold thy child.[12]

And as we practice this or some similar ritual from our own tradition, it will be fruitful to reflect on it in light of the *Ocean of Beauty*.

Verses, contemplations, chakras, pure sounds, yantras, rituals: by all these factors taken together, the *Ocean of Beauty* invites the worshiper to participate in a very complete encounter with the Goddess. It offers a way to maximize participation — in doing, hearing, seeing — for the sake of a heightened sense awareness that opens into an awareness of the total, all-encompassing presence of the Goddess in relation to the world and human self. The full human potential — to exist, to be conscious, to be joyful — is

---

12. From "The Blessed Virgin Compared to the Air We Breathe," Gerard Manley Hopkins, *Poems and Prose* (New York: Penguin Classics, 1985), 57–58.

brought to fruition, so that every experience becomes a Goddess-experience. Only personal limitations will then hinder the worshiper from seeing the Goddess in and as everything.

UNDERSTANDING RELIGIONS RELIGIOUSLY: WHAT RAMAKRISHNA REALIZED

The *Ocean of Beauty* invites the worshiper to experience the Goddess in an all-pervasive way. To worship her means also to resist limiting the divine to any one name or form or to any one aspect of human experience. To encounter her is to take into account all of one's spiritual resources, in all their particularity, and to trace their connection to the whole of the universe in all its parts. Feeling, acting, tasting, touching, hearing, seeing — all of this comes to mirror the unlimited greatness of the Goddess. Even the myth with which we began this chapter now falls into place, for both the totality of the gods' powers and the extreme violence of the buffalo demon are encompassed by the Goddess.

I would like to conclude this reflection on the Goddess and Goddess worship in the *Ocean of Beauty* by adding another insight which looks to the wider context. I have already mentioned Ramakrishna, the nineteenth-century holy man who worshiped the Goddess. His example and teaching highlight the Goddess as totalizing both world and self and as opening up a fruitful *religious* understanding of religious diversity. Once a person becomes aware of how the Goddess is the Mother who gives life to all reality, the world as we know it can be imagined as her body, as a sacred place or a series of chakras in which the worshiper opens gradually into divine consciousness.

The Great Master is one of the early and authoritative accounts of Ramakrishna's life. It describes the intuitive and planned experiments by which he sought to heighten his spiritual awareness, and how he explored a wide variety of spiritual pathways, all in relation to the Goddess whom he loved. *The Great Master* tells us that after years of intense devotion and spiritual discovery Ramakrishna concluded his experimentation by worshiping his wife, Sarada Devi, as the Goddess, an event mentioned earlier in this chapter. By this time he had already been exploring other religious traditions in India: devotion to Vishnu, the realization of the one true self in nondualist Vedanta, and Islam. But now he prays to his divine Mother to expand his horizons still further, and she responds by drawing him beyond his familiar Indian traditions. For he next turns to an encounter with Christianity:

After a year, the mind of the Master again looked forward to the vision of the divine Mother through another path. He had by that time become acquainted with Sambhuchandra Mallick, who read the Bible to him. Thus he came to know of the pure life of Jesus and of the faith he founded.[13]

But more was to follow: "Scarcely had that desire arisen in his mind when the divine Mother fulfilled it in a marvellous way and blessed him." He started meditating more regularly on Christ:

There were some good pictures hanging on the wall of that room. One of those pictures was that of the child Jesus in his mother's lap. The Master used to say that he sat one day in that parlour and was looking intently at that picture and thinking of the extraordinary life of Jesus, when he felt that the picture came to life, and effulgent rays of light, coming out from the bodies of the mother and the Child, entered into his heart and changed radically all the ideas in his mind! (*The Great Master,* 295)

He continued to meditate on Jesus and for a time became intensely devoted to Jesus alone; his experience culminated in what he knew to be a personal encounter with Jesus:

His love and devotion to the Gods and Goddesses vanished, and in their stead, a great faith in and reverence for Jesus and his religion occupied his mind, and began to show him Christian padrees offering incense and light before the image of Jesus in the Church and to reveal to him the eagerness of their hearts as is seen in their earnest prayers. The Master came back to the Dakshineswar temple and remained constantly absorbed in the meditation of those inner happenings. He forgot altogether to go to the temple of the divine Mother and pay obeisance to Her. The waves of those ideas had mastery over his mind in that manner for three days. At last, when the third day was about to close, the Master saw, while walking under the Panchavati, that a marvellous god-man of very fair complexion was coming toward him, looking steadfastly at him. As soon as the Master saw that person, he knew that he was a foreigner. He saw that his long eyes had produced a wonderful beauty in his face, and the tip of his nose, though a little

---

13. Swami Saradananda, *Sri Ramakrishna The Great Master,* trans. Swami Jagadananda (Madras: Sri Ramakrishna Math, 1952), 295.

flat, did not at all impair that beauty. The Master was charmed to see the extraordinary divine expression of that handsome face, and wondered who he was. Very soon the person approached him and from the bottom of the Master's pure heart came out with a ringing sound, the words, "Jesus! Jesus the Christ, the great Yogi, the loving Son of God, one with the Father, who gave his heart's blood and put up with endless torture in order to deliver men from sorrow and misery!" Jesus, the god-man, then embraced the Master and disappeared into his body and the Master entered into ecstasy, lost normal consciousness and remained identified for some time with the omnipresent Brahman with attributes. Having attained the vision of Jesus thus, the Master became free from the slightest doubt about Christ's having been an incarnation of God. (*The Great Master,* 295–96)

When Ramakrishna returned to ordinary consciousness he maintained the highest esteem for "Christ and his religion." Thereafter he always felt that he had had a real encounter with Christ; yet clearly this happened in a way that was based on his understanding of the Goddess and his sense of her pervasive presence in the world.

Ramakrishna seems to have recognized the world's religions as a spiritual gift, a series of interconnected opportunities for extending and deepening his spiritual experience. This larger religious world extended his primary religious experience and original encounter with the Goddess. To put it in my own words: it seems that the world became for him an arrangement of chakras, each religion a focal point for a particular kind of religious experience. By encountering the world religions in this way, Ramakrishna seemed to ascend through all religious possibilities to a complete realization of the Goddess he had known from the start.

A particular form of Hindu Goddess worship thus opened for him a perspective of universal relevance; it is worthwhile for us to reflect again on how very particular religious starting points can help us as we seek to encounter God in religious traditions other than our own. For instance, Christian reflection on other religions has taken a quite different course than Ramakrishna's, and it too is very particular in its roots. Yet Christians too have always sought to balance a very particular and concrete commitment to Christ with a sense of God's universal plan for the world. Indeed, many Christians say that their commitment to Christ is what makes it possible for them to see God's universal love filling the whole world. Even if Christians do not envision the world as a series of chakras, as Ramakrishna might, it is possible to say that Christians see the world as a single integral whole, perhaps even as a yantra centered on Christ who draws us into a vision of himself in the whole, and the whole in himself. Both patterns, chakra and yantra, can be helpful in imagining what we are doing when we learn from religious traditions other than our own — whether we see this learning as visiting a series of experiments to be worked through one after another (as if chakras), or as a single, continuous effort to see everything at once, gathered around its sacred center (as if a yantra or an icon). This book, for instance, could be usefully read according to either plan.

Once we are aware of the adjustments that have to be made, reflection on the *Ocean of Beauty* will make it easier for us to understand the grand, all-inclusive claim made in the Letter to the Colossians about Christ who is

> the image of the invisible God, the firstborn of all creation; for in him all things in heaven and on earth were created, things visible and invisible, whether thrones or dominions or rulers or powers — all things have been created through him and for him. He himself is before all things, and in him all things hold together. He is the head of the body, the church; he is the beginning, the firstborn from the dead, so that he might come to have first place in everything. For in him all the fullness of God was pleased to dwell, and through him God was pleased to reconcile to himself all things, whether on earth or in heaven, by making peace through the blood of his cross. (Col. 1:15–20)

So too, if we can understand how Ramakrishna could worship the Goddess and yet still enjoy every religious pathway, we may also be better able to grasp the dazzling vision of the world in Christ, again as envisioned by Hopkins:

> As kingfishers catch fire, dragonflies draw flame;
> As tumbled over rim in roundy wells
> Stones ring; like each tucked string tells, each hung bell's
> Bow swung finds tongue to fling out broad its name;
> Each mortal thing does one thing and the same:
> Deals out that being indoors each one dwells;
> Selves — goes itself; *myself* it speaks and spells,
> Crying *What I do is me: for that I came.*
>
> I say more: the just man justices;
> Keeps grace: that keeps all his goings graces;
> Acts in God's eye what in God's eye he is —

Christ — for Christ plays in ten thousand places,
Lovely in limbs, and lovely in eyes not his
To the Father through the features of men's faces.[14]

Seeing Christ everywhere, realizing all reality as pervaded by the Goddess: these achievements are very different from one another, yet it is valuable for us to consider both possibilities together, along with every other vision of religious wholeness we find around us.

The image of the Goddess presented in the *Ocean of Beauty* challenges us to deepen our spiritual roots and gain a deeper spiritual energy by which to ascend toward a full spiritual appreciation of the world in which we live. If we pay attention to life around us, we may find the energy and courage to open ourselves more completely to God who comes to us as our life, our energy, our death. This, Hindu wisdom tells us, is what it means to meet the Goddess.

14. *Poems and Prose,* Poem 34, p. 51.

7

Experimenting with Truth

Thinking about God can be a very satisfying human endeavor, and it can be exhausting or frightening; it may also seem to have been easier in ages past when the world seemed more religious, even a century ago when Ramakrishna lived. But a wise Hindu might suggest that we not worry or yearn for the past. True wisdom is available today; God is just as close to us now. Just take a careful look at yourself as you are, here and now, in everyday life, and you will find God. Just look humbly into the face of your neighbor, even your poorest neighbor, and there you will find God waiting for you. In this chapter, we explore what it means to know ourselves, face reality, and discover God in the modern world in which we live. Mohandas K. Gandhi and Mahasweta Devi will help us along the way.

We begin with Gandhi. When we think of him these days, it is difficult not to call to mind Attenborough's *Gandhi* and the startlingly fresh and clear presentation of Gandhi's life we see there: the bold and stubborn lawyer, freedom-fighter and teacher of nonviolence, icon of spiritual wisdom, martyr for religious tolerance and justice, father of independent India. A recent edition of his autobiography, *The Story of My Experiments with Truth,* even advertises it as "the book behind the movie." Even more than in his lifetime, Gandhi has become an enduring global figure, familiar to many who know nothing much else about Hinduism. So many years after his death in January 1948 he still inspires individuals in all parts of the world; his wisdom seems to be a practical wisdom for everyone.

Yet it is important to understand Gandhi in the context of his traditional Hindu culture, even if we do not wish to limit him to those origins. The early pages of his autobiography make clear that he grew up in a relatively traditional family. Throughout his life he cherished memories from his childhood, the traditional pieties and devotions, pious plays and stories, saintly individuals he met and read about. These would inspire him even many years later.

It is particularly interesting to view Gandhi in context because he was a Hindu with a twist. He remade the old in light of the new, yet without breaking the connections; he transformed Hindu wisdom and made it accessible in a new, wider world. Like many Hindus before him, he was a vegetarian and concerned about issues of diet, but for him diet and health also had to do with cultural identities and political power — were the British the rulers of India because they became strong through eating beef? Like many other Hindus, he believed in fasting, but when he fasted in public and for long periods of time, he made fasting a tool of consciousness-raising and civic transformation. He dressed simply, as would a traditional holy man, but made the point that plain homespun dress was good for indigenous Indian industries too. He spent a good bit of time thinking about the temples which were central to traditional Hindu piety, but his main concern was that every person, untouchables included, should be able to enter temples fearlessly and with dignity. He insisted that respect for cows is at the heart of Hinduism, but he also explained that these gentle and generous animals symbolize all that we need to affirm and learn about the animal world and the unity of all living beings. He understood the importance of pilgrimage in Hindu life, yet dramatically altered the destination of pilgrimage when he walked to the ocean to make salt and thus to contest the British power to impose taxes. He respected caste and insisted that caste distinctions had to be a part of future India, but only as a functional division of labor which could not be an excuse for demeaning anyone. Along with millions of other Hindus, he hoped to restore the ideal rule of the divine Rama, but this would now be a kingdom defined not primarily by political power but by speaking and acting the truth in all circumstances. And so on.

It is perhaps most interesting for us to note that he also strongly affirmed the importance of self-knowledge, which of course is one of the oldest values to which Hindus have adhered. Yet by his manner of search he also indicates, in a rather modern fashion, that the self is to be known according to its history, biographically, in the events and relationships of everyday life. All people are qualified to know the self, if they just pay close attention to what happens to them day by day, over the years.

In the following pages, let us consider more closely the way in which Gandhi searched his life experience and found there the basis for a thoroughly truthful and nonviolent way of life. After that, we will reflect more briefly on the writing of Mahasweta Devi, a contemporary author and social activist who explores what it means to live in India today, especially for those who are already marginalized due to gender or class or racial background.

THE EXPERIMENTAL LIFE

Gandhi wrote his autobiography little by little during the 1920s in a series of short chapters which were published serially as they were written. It is the work of a busy man who nevertheless felt it important to take the time to tell people about himself:

> I simply want to tell the story of my numerous experiments with truth, and as my life consists of nothing but those experiments, it is true that the story will take the shape of an autobiography. . . . I should certainly like to narrate my experiments in the spiritual field which are known only to myself, and from which I have derived such power as I possess for working in the political field. (*Experiments with Truth,* vi–vii)

Because Gandhi wants to show that his great themes of discipline, truth, and nonviolence are rooted in his everyday personal experience and that they can in fact be rooted in anyone's personal experience, he presents his story as a straightforward and practical account like anyone else's, a series of modest experiments in the practice of living:

> If I had only to discuss academic principles, I should clearly not at-tempt an autobiography. But my purpose is to give an account of various practical applications of these principles, so I have given the chapters I propose to write the title, *The Story of My Experiments with Truth.* . . . Let those who wish, realize how the conviction has grown on me; let them share my experiments and share my conviction, if they can. (*Experiments with Truth,* ix)

Throughout the autobiography Gandhi often dwells on details that are small, even seemingly trivial. But the stakes are high, since it is in this detailed and commonplace self-knowledge that one can see God:

> What I want to achieve — what I have been striving and pining to achieve these thirty years — is self-realization, to see God face to face, to attain Moksa [Liberation]. I live and move and have my being in pursuit of this goal. All that I do by way of speaking and writing,

and all my ventures in the political field, are directed to this same end. (*Experiments with Truth,* viii)

His "pining to see God" is of course not quite the same as the desire which afflicted Andal, whom we met in chapter 4, since Gandhi seeks a God who is first of all Truth:

> I worship God as Truth only. I have not yet found God, but I am seeking after God.... Often in my progress I have faint glimpses of the Absolute Truth, God; daily the conviction is growing upon me that He alone is real and all else unreal. (*Experiments with Truth,* ix)

By recollecting and examining how he had acted in the past, Gandhi became able to find his way back to the present moment, to a truth that is practical and present here and now. Since it is a lack of truth that increasingly twists relationships into violence, this discovery of truth also enabled him to live nonviolently and without fear in the face of violence.

To catch something of the wisdom that Gandhi offers us, let us examine four incidents from his life. Three come from the autobiography, while one is drawn from his *Satyagraha in South Africa.*

A TRUE CONFESSION

The autobiography contains many fascinating incidents from Gandhi's childhood and youth. He succeeds in showing us the deeper meaning of seemingly trivial incidents, such as why he tried eating meat and why he didn't cheat at school; and we learn much about him from poignant moments such as the death of his father and the events surrounding it. But most illuminating, I think, is the confession he makes to his father after he had stolen a bit of gold from his brother's bracelet. Though the theft could have gone unnoticed, afterward Gandhi began to feel so guilty that finally he had to make amends. He wrote a note to his father, confessing exactly what he had done. His father, who was ill, sat up in bed to read the note:

> He read the note through, and pearl-drops trickled down his cheeks, wetting the paper. For a moment he closed his eyes in thought and then tore up the note. He had sat up to read it. He again lay down. I also cried. I could see my father's agony. If I were a painter I could draw a picture of the whole scene today. It is still so vivid in my mind. Those pearl-drops of love cleansed my heart, and washed my sin away.

Only he who has experienced such love can know what it is. As the hymn says, "Only he who is smitten with the arrows of love knows its power." This sort of sublime forgiveness was not natural to my father. I had thought that he would be angry, say hard things, and strike his forehead.

He draws a lesson that will serve him well the rest of his life:

> But he was so wonderfully peaceful, and I believe this was due to my clean confession. A clean confession, combined with a promise never to commit the sin again, when offered before one who has the right to receive it, is the purest type of repentance. I know that my confession made my father feel absolutely safe about me, and increased his affection for me beyond measure. . . . This was, for me, an object-lesson in Nonviolence. Then I could read in it nothing more than a father's love, but today I know that it was pure Nonviolence. When such Nonviolence becomes all-embracing, it transforms everything it touches. There is no limit to its power. (*Experiments with Truth,* 23–24)[1]

In Gandhi's view, this experience was childhood testimony to the general principle that truth in word and deed will disarm even the most difficult situation and enable people to interact without fear and anger, nonviolently. He confessed, and his father not only forgave him but wept; years later, this moment would still guide the grown man in discovering the truth of every human situation, even when the fate of an empire was at stake.

LEAD, KINDLY LIGHT

Our second example occurs years later, when Gandhi was becoming increasingly involved in the struggle for the rights of Indians in South Africa, where he worked as a lawyer from 1893 to 1915. Then too, though he was very busy, he had time to explore and assess what was happening to him in his life. The following incident, recounted in *Satyagraha in South Africa,* illustrates how he found truth radiant in the details of his life.

When the British passed a registration act which required that Indians be registered and fingerprinted and carry identification papers with them at all times, Gandhi initially was the key figure in galvanizing the Indian community to resist registration. But after subtle negotiations with British officials,

---

1. Here and throughout, I substitute "Nonviolence" for Gandhi's *Ahimsa.*

he decided to trust them and agreed to a compromise: we Indians will register and even be fingerprinted if you then repeal the registration act. In this way, the community will show its respect for law, the government will save face, and in the end we will be freed from this odious law. Naturally, Gandhi had a hard time convincing his allies to agree to this unexpected change in position. But he insisted and even announced that he would be the very first to register. When he went out to do this, a strong and impetuous friend named Mir Alam came up to Gandhi and knocked him unconscious, to prevent him from registering. Gandhi's recollection of what happened next is illuminating.

As soon as he regained consciousness, his first concern was to insist that Mir Alam not be arrested and charged. He was, after all, just following his conscience. Later on Gandhi would comment that even if he had died due to the blow, nothing really would have been lost; in a true Satyagraha movement, where truth is grasped and the commitment to truth overcomes violence, everyone is a leader, no one is indispensable.

Despite his pain he remained determined to register and asked that the papers be brought immediately to his bedside. When Mr. Chamney, his key British adversary, came to see him, Gandhi painfully sat up, eager to register right away. As he registered, he noticed the Englishman's face and was struck at the softening of his adversary's heart:

> Mr. Chamney returned with the papers and I gave finger-prints, but not without pain. I then saw that tears stood in Mr. Chamney's eyes. I had often to write bitterly against him, but this showed me how man's heart may be softened by events.[2]

Being nonviolent and keeping one's word even in adversity enable people to step outside their antagonistic postures and deal sincerely and humanely with one another.

After this Gandhi is taken for recuperation to the house of a Rev. Dokes. Recalling the family's hospitality gives him occasion to recollect an earlier discussion in which he had worried that it was perhaps imprudent for Dokes to be involved in the struggle for Indian rights, since he might in that way offend his European benefactors. But this hesitation elicits an eloquent protest from Dokes:

> My dear friend, what do you think of the religion of Jesus? I claim to be a humble follower of Him who cheerfully mounted the cross for

---

2. *Satyagraha in South Africa,* trans. Valji G. Desai (Ahmedabad: Navajivan Publishing House, 1928), 170.

the faith that was in Him, and whose love was as wide as the world. I must take a public part in your struggle if I am at all desirous of representing Christ to the Europeans who, you are afraid, will give me up as punishment for it. And I must not complain if they do thus give me up. My livelihood is indeed derived from them, but you certainly do not think that I am associated with them for a living's sake, or that they are my cherishers. My cherisher is God; they are but instruments of His Almighty Will. It is one of the unwritten conditions of my connection with them, that none of them may interfere with my religious liberty. (*Satyagraha in South Africa,* 172)

Gandhi rightly appreciated this remarkable confession of core religious beliefs as a testimony which crossed religious boundaries. In his mind, his reaction to injury and Dokes's courageous loyalty were both ordinary deeds such as anyone could perform, evidence of the universal power of truth to transform violence into harmony.

While he was resting at the Dokeses' house, he asked their daughter to sing his favorite hymn, "Lead, Kindly Light." That Gandhi resonated so well with this particular hymn reminds us that he was not favored with great visions of God, but only small glimpses, one at a time:

> Lead, kindly Light, amid th'encircling gloom,
>   Lead Thou me on:
> The night is dark, and I am far from home,
>   Lead Thou me on!
> Keep Thou my feet! I do not ask to see
> The distant scene; one step enough for me.
>
> I was not ever thus, nor prayed that Thou
>   Shouldst lead me on;
> I loved to choose and see my path; but now
>   Lead Thou me on!
> I loved the garish day; and spite of fears,
> Pride ruled my will: remember not past years.
>
> So long Thy power hath blest me, sure it still
>   Will lead me on
> O'er moor and fen, o'er crag and torrent, till
>   The night is gone;
> And with the morn those angel faces smile,
> Which I have loved long since, and lost awhile.

Charles Andrews, another Christian friend, records that once, at their ashram near Durban, South Africa, Gandhi asked him to sing "Lead, Kindly Light." Andrews sings, while all listen in prayerful silence; he remembers looking at Gandhi:

> Even then, though he was much younger, his frail body was worn with suffering that could never be laid aside even for a moment: yet his spirit within was radiant when the hymn broke the silence, with its solemn close, "And with the morn those angel faces smile, Which I have loved long since, and lost awhile." I can remember how we all sat in silence when the hymn was finished, and how he then repeated to himself those two lines which I have quoted.[3]

Despite Gandhi's insistence that his goal was to see God, he seems to have spent his life in a kind of spiritual twilight, knowing only a step at a time where events would lead him. He was not a visionary; he had no special revelations. He records his steps in the dark without seeking spiritual privilege or favor and shows that remaining faithful to truth in daily life is the surest way to God.

Gandhi concludes his account of the registration by admitting that there is much in the chapter that will seem irrelevant. A few pages later, he adds honestly but bleakly that the British reneged on the deal and did not remove the requirement of registration. The whole incident, from the legal quarrel with the British to Gandhi's injury and all that followed, did not add up to any momentous accomplishment; yet when he probed it he still found it rich with insights into how truth, nonviolence, and glimpses of God are woven together in a life honestly and courageously lived.

WRITING THE TRUTH

Our third example takes us back to the autobiography, to a chapter entitled, "Intimate European Contacts." Near the middle of his book, Gandhi stops and admits that neither political action nor soul-searching nor writing come easily to him. He confesses that usually he has had to rely on the religious wisdom of others, but even then remained inarticulate about God:

> I have not seen God, neither have I known him. I have made the world's faith in God my own, and as my faith is ineffaceable, I re-

---

3. *The Gandhi Reader*, ed. Homer A. Jack (Bloomington: Indiana University Press, 1956), 391.

gard that faith as amounting to experience. However, as it may be said that to describe faith as experience is to tamper with truth, it may perhaps be more correct to say that I have no words for characterizing my belief in God. (*Experiments with Truth,* 246)

He explains how he manages to write in such ambiguous circumstances:

I write just as the Spirit moves me at the time of writing. I do not claim to know definitely that all conscious thought and action on my part is directed by the Spirit. But on an examination of the greatest steps that I have taken in my life, as also of those that may be regarded as the least, I think it will not be improper to say that all of them were directed by the Spirit. It is perhaps now somewhat easy to understand why I believe that I am writing this story as the Spirit prompts me. (*Experiments with Truth,* 246)

Indeed, in a simple aside that authors do well to ponder at length, he adds that even his writing is itself a religious activity: "Writing this is itself one of my experiments with truth" (*Experiments with Truth,* 247).

Gandhi illustrates his manner of self-scrutiny and confessional writing somewhat indirectly by drawing attention to the ordering of chapters in this part of the autobiography. He explains why this chapter, "Intimate European Contacts," follows the one that now precedes it in the text, "A Sacred Recollection and a Penance." He says that he had intended to write first about his "Intimate European Contacts," but found that he was unable to do so until he had dealt with other issues. He therefore had to stop and first write about "A Sacred Recollection and a Penance."

Gandhi begins "A Sacred Recollection and a Penance" by observing that he has always gotten along well with Indians of diverse backgrounds and relates easily to both relatives and strangers, countrymen and foreigners, people of white and mixed racial backgrounds, Hindus and Indians of other faiths. Meeting different kinds of people was actually much easier for him than practicing the virtues of nonviolence, celibacy, and nonpossessiveness.

These comments serve to introduce a less pleasant incident that occurred when he was still practicing law full time. It seems that his law clerks were living with him in his house, and among other practical signs of hospitality, he and his wife, Kasturbhai, would take down their chamber pots each morning. When she balks at taking down the pot for a low-caste Christian, Gandhi insists; she relents, though with tears. He is very much annoyed at her tears, since he believes that duty must be done cheerfully. He undertakes to correct her, and they begin to argue; in the heat of their argument he even drags her to the gate, threatening to expel her from his house. She protests,

> Have you no sense of shame? Must you so far forget yourself? Where am I to go? I have no parents or relatives here to harbor me. Being your wife, you think I must put up with your cuffs and kicks? For heaven's sake, behave yourself, and shut the gate. Let us not be found making scenes like this! (*Experiments with Truth*, 244)

Gandhi is chastened; he relents and they are reconciled. In writing about the incident he says that at that time he still viewed Kasturbhai as an object of lust, an object of his bad and good desires, be it sexual desire or anger or even a well-intentioned plan to improve her. He admits that in the intervening years he has learned to let her think differently and even disagree with him; indeed, they reach a point where they no longer discuss politics at all.

It is only after this odd personal interlude that he can finally take up his original topic, "Intimate European Contacts." The chamber pot incident is a small one, but it is striking that years later he was still reflecting on that confrontation with Kasturbhai and saw fit to include it in the autobiography. The pattern is highly instructive: before he speaks of his European acquaintances, he needs to say that he gets along well with his fellow Indians; before he speaks of them, he needs to confess how difficult it was to practice virtue; and before this, he must add that he had trouble getting along with his own wife. Only then can he write the passages from "Intimate European Contacts" which I quoted above, about not seeing God clearly and about writing as the Spirit moves him. In light of his confession about Kasturbhai, it becomes all the more pointed that several pages later he should describe writing itself as a nonviolent act.

At the end of the autobiography Gandhi reaffirms that his goal has been simply to tell the truth and thus to speak of God:

> My uniform experience has convinced me that there is no other God than Truth. And if every page of these chapters does not proclaim to the reader that the only means for the realization of Truth is Nonviolence, I shall deem all my labor in writing these chapters to have been in vain.... To describe the Truth, as it has appeared to me, and in the exact manner in which I have arrived at it, has been my ceaseless effort. The exercise has given me ineffable mental peace, because it has been my fond hope that it might bring faith in Truth and Nonviolence to waverers. (*Experiments with Truth*, 453)

We saw in chapter 4 that in the *Gita* Arjuna finally saw Krishna face to face. But Gandhi sees only the little that is reflected in the mirror of daily life; even in the end he has only a glimpse of God:

> The little fleeting glimpses, therefore, that I have been able to have of Truth can hardly convey an idea of the indescribable lustre of Truth, a million times more intense than that of the sun we daily see with our eyes. In fact what I have caught is only the faintest glimmer of that mighty effulgence. (*Experiments with Truth,* 454)

This is to be expected from the man whose favorite hymn was "Lead, Kindly Light," a hymn about not seeing God, about walking in the dark, one step at a time. Though he was a true believer, Gandhi's faith was experimental, based not in extraordinary vision but in the work of daily life, in ordinary commitments faithfully and honestly lived.

SEEING GOD FACE TO FACE, AMONG THE POOR

But once Gandhi did claim to see God, a claim that must be put in context. Our fourth and briefest example is drawn from Gandhi's account of the short period when he worked in the town of Champaran in north India in a "bold experiment in Truth and Nonviolence" (*Experiments with Truth,* 274). He went to Champaran to help the desperately poor indigo workers. They were caught in the vicious cycle of the *tinkathia* system; i.e., 15 percent of the land leased to them had to be planted with indigo, for the benefit of their landlords. Devotion of this much land to a cash crop meant that they could never grow enough food to feed their families for the year. In Champaran Gandhi engaged in the basic work of collecting grievances, legal evidence, and signatures; he also got involved in other good works, such as arranging for the building of schools and clinics. He was successful enough in all of this to become unpopular with the British officials in the area, but despite their best efforts to evict him from Champaran, he refused to go. Public pressure and peaceful noncooperation with the authorities had their reward, and finally Gandhi won the right to stay. He was enthused by the success and proclaimed that "the country thus had its first direct object-lesson in Civil Disobedience." In the end, the campaign succeeded and the system of *tinkathia* was repealed. But ever careful to tell the truth and not to exaggerate his success, Gandhi adds that when he departed many other tasks — such as the building projects and the cow protection program — were left incomplete, and many of them remain forever unfinished, like "castles in the air."

But for Gandhi the enduring value of his Champaran experience rested on an insight that occurred at the very beginning of his visit. When he arrived he was joyfully welcomed by the workers, without fear about reprisals from those in power. Gandhi interpreted the exhilarating moment as a consummate verification of his belief that God and truth and nonviolence are inseparable:

> It is no exaggeration, but the literal truth, to say that in this meeting with the peasants I was face to face with God, Nonviolence and Truth. When I come to examine my title to this realization, I find nothing but my love for the people. And this in turn is nothing but an expression of my unshakable faith in Nonviolence. That day in Champaran was an unforgettable event in my life and a red-letter day for the peasants and for me. (*Experiments with Truth,* 369–70)

Gandhi was not the kind of person to seek God in yogic meditation or in temple worship; he never claimed any special vision of God; he did not present himself as a pious devotee or wise philosopher. It was in the faces of the poor that he had his best glimpse of God: at long last he was face to face.

At the end of the autobiography he emphasizes that finding God, doing the truth, and living the nonviolent life belong together. This insight shapes his understanding of politics and religion:

> But this much I can say with assurance, as a result of all my experiments, that a perfect vision of Truth can only follow a complete realization of Nonviolence. To see the universal and all-pervading Spirit of Truth face to face one must be able to love the meanest of creation as oneself. And a man who aspires after that cannot afford to keep out of any field of life. That is why my devotion to Truth has drawn me into the field of politics; and I can say without the slightest hesitation, and yet in all humility, that those who say that religion has nothing to do with politics do not know what religion means. (*Experiments with Truth,* 453–54)

Right action, experimentation with self, the discovery of self in the practicalities of daily life: these are his steps toward God, and these offer yet another aspect of Hindu wisdom, one that is particularly relevant even now, at the beginning of the twenty-first century.

There are many ways that we might enrich our appreciation of Gandhi's wisdom, beginning of course with reflection on our own life stories and the times in our lives when we had been faced with a choice between truth and violence. We might find inspiration in the life stories of people in our own traditions who have walked the same path as Gandhi, in their own ways, figures as diverse as Martin Luther King, the Dalai Lama, Archbishop Romero. Whenever I read Gandhi, I am reminded of Dorothy Day (1897–1980), the American woman who, with Peter Maurin, founded the Catholic Worker. She too put into practice the most basic values of nonviolence and solidarity with the poor; she too searched her soul and wrote movingly of how she received a gracious wisdom that made it possible for her to live fully, to have a baby, to become a Catholic. Her autobiography is entitled *The Long Loneliness,* and this is the way it concludes:

> We were just sitting there talking when Peter Maurin came in.
>
> We were just sitting there talking when lines of people began to form, saying, "We need bread." We could not say, "Go, be thou filled." If there were six small loaves and a few fishes, we had to divide them. There was always bread.
>
> We were just sitting there talking and people moved in on us. Let those who can take it, take it. Some moved out and that made room for more. And somehow the walls expanded.
>
> We were just sitting there talking and someone said, "Let's all go live on a farm."
>
> It was as casual as all that, I often think. It just came about. It just happened.
>
> I found myself, a barren woman, the joyful mother of children. It is not easy always to be joyful, to keep in mind the duty of delight.
>
> The most significant thing about *The Catholic Worker* is poverty, some say.
>
> The most significant thing is community, others say. We are not alone any more.
>
> But the final word is love. At times it has been, in the words of Father Zossima, a harsh and dreadful thing, and our very faith in love has been tried through fire.
>
> We cannot love God unless we love each other, and to love we must know each other. We know Him in the breaking of bread, and we are not alone anymore. Heaven is a banquet and life is a banquet, too, even with a crust, where there is companionship. We have all known the long loneliness and we have learned that the only solution is love and that love comes with community.
>
> It all happened while we sat there talking, and it is still going on.[4]

---

4. From Dorothy Day, *The Long Loneliness: An Autobiography* (San Francisco: HarperSan-Francisco, 1981), 285–86.

Gandhi would have resonated very well with her commitments, her non-violence, her sense of the interplay of community and loneliness, and he would have appreciated her ability to write from that experience. Like the best of Hindu wisdom, his truth opened upon realities that could be found and affirmed in other places, other lives, other confessions.

WOMEN'S BODIES, WOMEN'S TRUTHS— ACCORDING TO MAHASWETA DEVI

Now let us look beyond Gandhi. For it would be a mistake to imagine India's religious history or Hindu wisdom to have come to an end with him. Even in his own time, Gandhi was one among many figures with ideas about how the Hindu tradition should renew itself in the new world context. Since Independence some have tried faithfully and sensibly to follow Gandhi's agenda, working toward an inclusive India not divided by religious boundaries. There have likewise always been Hindus who vehemently reject Gandhi's mix of tradition and adaptation, and there are many strands of contemporary Hindu identity that do not depend directly on Gandhi at all.

In keeping with our approach to Gandhi, however, I wish to offer just one example from India's still growing store of wisdom, how an Indian living today has sought to use writing in an active and forceful way, so as to reveal the true nature of Indian life, including religious life. I am thinking of Mahasweta Devi, the Bengali activist and writer born in 1926.

Like Gandhi, Mahasweta Devi has dedicated herself to people in need. In particular she has focused her attention on the plight of tribal people, the indigenous inhabitants of India who have never been fully integrated into the wider Indian society, who have been marginalized and exploited in many ways; from among those, she has tried particularly to understand the experience of tribal women. Mahasweta is an activist who has undertaken many forms of community organizing in order to protect tribals from violence against them — religious and social, economic and political, even governmental. Her consistent goal has been to enable tribals to interact and work more closely together, wherever they live in India. For this purpose she has founded several organizations, e.g., the Lodha Organization (1978), the Bonded Labor Liberation Organization (1979), and the Tribal Unity Forum (1986). She has persistently kept after governmental agencies, targeting officials in key positions of power. So determined is she in her letter-writing that in one interview she muses that some officials have done the right thing simply to avoid getting more letters from her. Like Gandhi, she is a journalist, writing regular newspaper columns. She too has sought to put herself on the line, choosing to live with tribals in order to see the world through their eyes and to write from that perspective.[5]

Thanks to the translations and critical essays of Gayatri Spivak, Mahasweta Devi is becoming known in the West as activist, critic, and above all as a writer of short stories. These stories provide scenarios, fictional but clearly based in experience, which make the honest reader face up to the violence and falsehood still evident in modern society. They are rich, multifaceted, and liable to multiple interpretations; in the following paragraphs I draw out a spiritual meaning for them, but do not venture to claim that I have discovered their single correct meaning.

In these stories, she pushes Indian society to confront the falsehood and violence of its own history and particularly to look directly at the suffering of its concealed and marginalized members. When Gandhi scrutinized his own life experience, everything was ultimately a question of self, his particular story and the universal truths that could guide every human being. Mahasweta pursues similar purposes, for she too seeks interconnection and transformation; but, if I may make a basic distinction, it seems that she focuses less on "self" and more on "the other," the neglected outsider who cannot be encompassed or predicted by my self-understanding. Gandhi could be brutally honest in examining his own life, his relationships and accomplishments. Mahasweta speaks much less about herself, but is vigorous in putting the marginalized before herself and her readers, so that these forgotten people can no longer be passed over in silence. Let us look briefly at several of her stories.

In "Douloti the Beautiful" we are introduced to the plight of bonded laborers who work endlessly for their masters, ever accumulating debts that can never be paid back. As the story begins, we see the brutal injury of a father forced to pull a heavy cart in the noonday sun because his life is more expendable than that of a valued bullock. We follow his plight and see how his new destitution forces him to allow the "marriage" of his young daughter, Douloti, to a man from the city — who promptly sells her to a house of prostitution.

The story goes on to describe in excruciating detail the decline and degradation of Douloti, who is caught in a system that grinds her down. She is not an idealized, all-knowing victim who finds redemption in her suffering; she does not even seem to understand what is happening to her. The setting could just as well have been Gandhi's Champaran; altruistic reporters and

---

5. Some information about Mahasweta Devi can be found in the preface and introductory interview with her in *Imaginary Maps: Three Stories by Mahasweta Devi* (New York: Routledge, 1995).

social workers, aspiring to Gandhian ideals, keep visiting the town where Douloti is kept. But all their work is for nought; whatever slim structural changes might be set in place can do nothing during the shortened life of this one woman, Douloti.

Weakened by disease and abuse, Douloti becomes useless to her owners, and she is finally "freed" from the house of prostitution. She wanders about, near death, until she finds a cool, swept place in a schoolyard; she lies down there in the dark, and dies. It turns out that the next day is Independence Day. When Mohan, the village schoolteacher, and his students come to the school in the morning, they are dismayed to discover Douloti's corpse lying sprawled across the map of India which they had carefully drawn in preparation for the day's festivities:

> Filling the entire Indian peninsula from the oceans to the Himalayas, here lies bonded labor spread-eagled, kamiya-whore Douloti Nagesia's tormented corpse, putrefied with venereal disease, having vomited up all the blood in its desiccated lungs. Today, on the fifteenth of August, Douloti has left no room at all in the India of people like Mohan for planting the standard of the Independence flag. What will Mohan do now? Douloti is all over India. ("Douloti," 93)[6]

Violence is uncovered, the harsh truth revealed. Mahasweta does not moralize in Gandhi's fashion, but clearly she believes that it is valuable to see reality just as it is, in all its untruth and violence. But she leaves it to readers to decide whether they will keep looking, or just turn away.

The power of uncovering reality in all its violence is most vividly shown in another story about a woman in trouble. The woman is named Draupadi, after the heroine of the *Mahabharata* who was saved from the humiliation of being stripped publicly only by the intervention of Krishna. In the story, Draupadi is a tribal activist involved in a regional insurgency. After her closest comrade is killed, she is captured by the crafty police official Senanayak; he is an expert on tribals, known for his astute grasp of the tribal mentality. He has her "prepared" for interrogation by a night of torture and gang rape; later on, the plan is, she will be disposed of and listed as "countered," killed in an encounter with the police. When the time comes for her interrogation by Senanayak, he orders that she be cleaned up and dressed and brought before him; he does not want to see the violence that has been inflicted on her. But she tears up the clothing given her, she refuses to be clothed; still bloody,

---

6. "Douloti the Beautiful," as translated by Gayatri Spivak in *Imaginary Maps.*

she strides naked into Senanayak's presence. Literally, she lays bare the truth of the situation, the violence endemic in his clever police campaign:

> Draupadi stands before him, naked. Thigh and pubic hair matted with dry blood. Two breasts, two wounds. "What is this?," he is about to bark. Draupadi comes closer. Stands with her hand on her hip, laughs and says, "The object of your search, Draupadi Mejhen. You asked them to make me up, don't you want to see how they made me?" "Where are her clothes?" "Won't put them on, sir. Tearing them."[7]

She is no classical Draupadi, for no deity intervenes to help or cover her; rather, she has become like the Goddess Kali in all her dark terrifying power as she taunts this latter-day demon general:

> Draupadi's black body comes closer. Draupadi shakes with an indomitable laughter that Senanayak simply cannot understand. Her ravaged lips bleed as she begins laughing. Draupadi wipes the blood on her palm and says in a voice that is as terrifying, sky splitting, and sharp as her ululation, "What's the use of clothes? You can strip me, but how can you clothe me again? Are you a man?"

For the first time in his life, Senanayak is afraid. He backs away; he has seen too much:

> She looks around and chooses the front of Senanayak's white bush shirt to spit a bloody gob at and says, "There isn't a man here that I should be ashamed. I will not let you put my cloth on me. What more can you do? Come on, counter me, counter me — come on, counter me!" Draupadi pushes Senanayak with her two mangled breasts, and for the first time Senanayak is afraid to stand before an unarmed target, terribly afraid. ("Draupadi," 196)

This is truth, a truth manifest and thrown back into the face of violence. In my reading, this is a kind of Goddess-theophany, now in a contemporary situation devoid of settled religious signs and explanations. It is raw, untreated, unmediated truth, and it is distinctively Mahasweta's; though Gandhi's reflective apprehension of truth too was meant to confront and reverse violence, it is different in form and feel from hers: Mahasweta assigns

---

7. "Draupadi," as translated by Gayatri Spivak in *In Other Worlds* (New York: Routledge, 1988), 196.

no meaning to what she sees and shows; she is content simply to uncover the spectacle, and lets the reader find what wisdom may lie there.

NOWHERE A SPECTATOR

As writer, journalist, novelist, she draws readers into the contemporary reality they may have managed to ignore or consider only in theory. In a long story entitled "Pterodactyl, Puran Sahay, and Pirtha," Mahasweta again turns to the plight of the tribals, this time by having a well-meaning journalist named Puran Sahay — a kind of Gandhi, a Mahasweta Devi — attempt to trace down the mysterious rumors of the reappearance of the prehistoric pterodactyl bird in the tribal area of Pirtha. He cannot find the bird — perhaps it is simply a boy's tale — but he eventually realizes that the tribals themselves are like some dinosaur passing through modern India: rare, almost invisible, out of place. When encountered, the tribals too are unable to speak in the language of the modern world; communication has been so rare, for so long, that a common language no longer exists.

At the end of this story, though, Mahasweta seems to hold out a possibility of hope, at least indicating what needs to be done if hope is to become possible again:

Only love, a tremendous, excruciating, explosive love can still dedicate us to this work when the century's sun is in the western sky. Otherwise, this aggressive civilization will have to pay a terrible price. Look at history, how aggressive civilizations have destroyed themselves in the name of progress, every time. Love, excruciating love — let that be the first step. Puran thus discovered what love there was in his heart for the land of Pirtha. Perhaps now he could no longer remain a distant spectator, anywhere in life. ("Pterodactyl," 196)

These words describe her basic commitment, and Gandhi's as well: to speak, write, act in such a way that truth is uncovered, that severed, denied human relationships are presented for reconsideration and possibly healed. Her goal is to implicate everyone who comes by, making it impossible to view reality from a safe distance: "Perhaps now he could no longer remain a distant spectator, anywhere in life." The writer is involved and involves others.

Surely this must be our goal too, if we are to be good readers, if we are to honor the memory of Gandhi and listen seriously to Mahasweta. If we too are rediscovering religious wisdom in today's world, we too must move beyond genial truths which can neither be verified nor proven wrong and seek a richer, living truth in the midst of life. What matters most is that we become involved, implicated in what happens around us, risking ourselves while learning to include the stranger in our midst; we need to become familiar with what is alien and frightening to us, and in the process reintegrate our original selves.

By this program the self is discovered through an honest appropriation of the world around us in all its diversity; in a way, it thus reverses and yet validates the process of creation which we considered in chapter 1, where the original self became many:

> Now the Person was of the same size and kind as a man and woman closely embracing. He caused himself to fall into two parts, and from him a husband and wife were born. Therefore the sage Yajnavalkya said, "By oneself, one is like a half-fragment"; but this space is filled by woman. He united with her, and thus humankind was born. But the woman reflected, "How can he unite with me after engendering me from himself? For shame! I will conceal myself."

We find our way back through violence and shame, back to the original interconnectedness of things. Perhaps this is Mahasweta's contribution to Hindu wisdom, a way to glimpse divine realities at the end of this century.

ALONE, LIKE GOD

Let us consider just one more story, "The Wet Nurse," the tale of another woman with a significant name. She is Yashoda, surely a reminder to the Hindu reader of the quintessential Indian mother, Yashoda, who cared for young Krishna. This latter-day Yashoda is the wife of a brahmin in Calcutta who is run over by the reckless son of Halderbabu, a rich merchant. Her husband is crippled for life, his sacred brahmin feet no longer useful for anything at all, except as an entirely inert object of traditional reverence. To compensate for her husband's disability, Yashoda makes use of her own best physical asset — her large and very generous breasts. These breasts have amazing capacity and are so generous in giving milk that she can breast-feed her own twenty children, and then some thirty more children from the rich Halder clan. This service brings in money and provides food for her husband and children; it also allows the younger Halders to keep producing children as they wish, husbands sure that their wives, freed from the need to breast-feed, will forever keep their comely feminine form. Surrogate for everyone else, Yashoda is the quintessential mother, the ultimate female principle, as

Mahasweta puts it in these words that are rich in tradition and dripping with sarcasm:

> Yashoda was a true example of Indian womanhood. She was typical of a chaste and loving wife and devoted mother, ideals which defy intelligence and rational explanation, which involve sacrifice and dedication stretching the limits of imagination, and which have been kept alive in the popular Indian psyche through the ages.... Seeing such a woman, every Tom, Dick and Harry knows that the ancient Indian traditions are alive and kicking. Old sayings celebrating the fortitude of women were made to describe such females. Actually, Yashoda did not wish to blame her husband one bit for their calamity. The same protective love that welled up within Yashoda for her children reached out to envelop her husband. She wanted to be transformed into an Earth Mother, rich in a harvest of fruits and grains, in order to feed her disabled husband and helpless children. The ancient sages have depicted man and woman as the male and female principles in nature.

Everyone takes advantage of Yashoda, at the same time honoring her with a mythic status which safely — safely for them — distances her from their real lives:

> But they never described this maternal emotion that Yashoda felt toward her husband. After all, the sages existed in those long-forgotten times when they first came into India from other countries — but such is the chemistry of the soil of this land that all women turn into mothers here, and all men choose to be eternal sons. ("The Wet Nurse," 33–34)[8]

After Yashoda's extraordinary maternal capacity has been thoroughly exploited, her fortunes wane; the story goes on to chart her decline, her diminished ability to produce milk, and the decay of her physical attractiveness. She is used up, sucked dry. Her decline is matched by her husband's infidelity and the growing coldness of the large Halder family. Made into a commodity, she no longer matters when her productivity ends. She develops breast cancer; it is neglected, and she does not say anything about it until it is too late. Finally she is left alone to die in a hospital ward in the middle of the night:

---

8. "The Wet Nurse," as translated by Ella Dutta in *Truth Tales* (New York: Feminist Press at the City University of New York, 1990), 25–62. See also Gayatri Spivak's translation of the story in *In Other Worlds.*

Whatever Yashoda had thought had come true. She was like God in this respect: whatever was in her mind was executed by others. This time also was no exception, for Yashoda's death was God's death. In this world, it has always happened that when a person takes Godhood upon herself, she is rejected by everyone and left to die alone. ("The Wet Nurse," 61–62)

Does Mahasweta mean that Yashoda is God, a Goddess? Maybe, maybe not; Mahasweta's views of religion are elusive. But there is a sub-plot in "The Wet Nurse," in which the local temple Goddess is likewise reduced to a pawn in the hands of unscrupulous temple priests. Perhaps the reader is being prompted to read Yashoda's story as a religious tale, and the Goddess's tale as a woman's tale: women, divine and human, are all misused. As Mahasweta herself has indicated, even "Mother India" herself is misused, used, abused, sucked dry.[9] God, whoever God may be, is there in the same darkness where Yashoda lies forgotten.

At the end of this century, some of us find ourselves in that same darkness where Gandhi walked as he murmured the words of "Lead, Kindly Light"; the spiritual path is not clear, wisdom elusive. We may also share something of this modern Yashoda's experience, as we face the dark alone, by ourselves, like a God who stands alone in the beginning, potentially everything and everyone. It is Hindu wisdom to note that no beginning is ever the first of all beginnings; it is also wise to recognize that a confrontation with ultimate loneliness is never the last of all endings. When we hear about Yashoda — "In this world, it has always happened that when a person takes Godhood upon herself, she is rejected by everyone and left to die alone" — we find ourselves back where we started in chapter 1:

In the beginning, this universe was self, in the form of Person. The Person looked around and saw nothing other than himself. First the Person said, "I am," and thus the word "I" originated. Therefore, even now, when addressed a person first responds, "I am," and afterward says whatever other name he has. . . . The Person was afraid, and therefore whoever is all alone is afraid. But the Person reflected, "Since there is nothing other than me, of what am I afraid?" Then his fear vanished, for of what could he have been afraid? One becomes afraid only of someone else. But neither did he rejoice, for one who is all alone does not rejoice. The Person desired a second.

---

9. See the essay about "Breast-Giver" in *In Other Worlds,* where Spivak reports both Mahasweta's own interpretation of the story and other views of it.

The possibility is there: in the isolation of the self, however this may be explained, there is once again a desire for something more. The world can always be created again, it must begin again, life is not exhausted. This insight too must be internalized in the creative process by which the self makes its world, encompasses everything that seems other to it and surrenders to that other, thereby finding itself anew. So there is no ending to our story, and the patient reader might finish this book by returning to chapter 1 and starting over again, reflecting on how the self finds and creates and surpasses itself. But now we can do this with a richer awareness, for we have encountered a Hindu wisdom as old as the beginning, as timely as tomorrow, as personal and familiar as my own self.

8

A Final Word on the Wisdom of Watching and Waiting

As I finished writing this book I was also reading the *Showings* of Julian of Norwich, the fourteenth-century Christian mystic. *Showings* is the story of what God revealed to Julian when she seemed near death at age thirty. A priest came and placed a crucifix before her as she lay in her bed, and over a day and night she glimpsed many aspects of God's wisdom and love as these were shown her in the crucified Jesus. She tells her readers how she was graced to be able to look long and steadily upon that face, observing with compassion and gratitude how much he suffered for her and how much he loved her. She was deeply moved:

And when I was thirty and a half years old, God sent me a bodily sickness in which I lay for three days and three nights, and on the third night I received all the rites of Holy Church, and did not expect to live until day.... My curate was sent for to be present at my end; and before he came my eyes were fixed upward, and I could not speak. He set the cross before my face, and said, "I have brought the image of your savior; look at it, and take comfort from it...." Then suddenly it came into my mind that I ought to wish for the second wound as a gift and a grace from our Lord, that my body might be filled full of recollection and feeling of his blessed Passion, as I had prayed before; for I wished that his pains be my pains, with compassion which would lead to longing for God.[1]

---

1. Julian of Norwich, *Showings*, trans. Edmund Colledge, O.S.A., and James Walsh, S.J., (Mahwah, N.J.: Paulist Press, 1978), Long Text, 179–80.

During the ensuing day and night Julian was shown different aspects and nuances of the suffering and love of Christ, of God and the human condition; she faced the enormities of suffering and sin, the even greater abundance of divine love and grace, and peered into her own deepest self as God saw her.

In her encounter with Christ Julian was able to understand the meaning of love; she saw the wideness of God's plan for her and the whole world. By seeing things just as they are, without romance and in the presence of Christ, she began to see the gracious goodness which pervades all reality. She realized that even the things and people she could not understand and account for were also being kept safe by God, for all things will be well:

> Because of the tender love which our good Lord has for all who will be saved, he comforts readily and sweetly, and he means this: "It is true that sin is the cause of all this pain, but all will be well, and every kind of thing will be well. . . . " In these same words I saw hidden in God an exalted and wonderful mystery, which he will make plain and we shall know in heaven. (*Showings*, 225–26)

When she had recovered, she wrote an initial account of her visions. Then, for a period of twenty years, she kept meditating on what she had seen, and finally rewrote her account, this time even more deeply infused with insights into the mystery of God's grace and plan for the world:

> And from the time that it was revealed, I desired many times to know in what was our Lord's meaning. Fifteen years and more later, I was answered in spiritual understanding, and it was said, "What, do you wish to know your Lord's meaning in this thing? Know it well, love was his meaning. Who reveals it to you? Love. What did he reveal to you? Love. Why does he reveal it to you? For love. Remain in this, and you will know more of the same. But you will never know different, without end." So I was taught that love is our Lord's meaning. (*Showings*, 342)

Over those intervening years, Julian had learned to take deeply to heart what she had seen and to live a life that was never turned away from what God had shown her. She saw only Christ, but she saw everything in Christ, and she knew that it was God's will to make all things well, infused with love.

Why do I mention this? At the end of a book like this, we might think that an intense focus on Christ or on any specific religious figure would be an obstacle to learning from the religious wisdom of India, as if too much particularity would make us narrow and closed. But Julian can be a model for us, as we learn to see everything in light of that which we most love and cherish. We too need to deepen our first loves, and then we need to spend time with Hindu wisdom, to live with it for a time before we decide how best to learn from it. We need to contemplate how God has been acting in our lives thus far, so that we can also see with a fresh eye all that God is showing us today. In this way, over the years, we can learn to see God in ourselves and our world, and in the wisdom which comes to us from India and other places too. Like Julian, we need to be willing to spend a long time at this, watching with our eyes wide open until everything is made clear and nothing remains hidden, as we realize that even now God is making all things well.

In the experiments which make up the preceding chapters I have been inviting the reader to drink deeply of the wisdom of the Hindu religious traditions and on that basis to envision more broadly what we are about in trying to live wisely today. This is a spiritual task, for people who want to flourish and live full spiritual lives. Those of us who are Christian can keep looking upon the face of Christ, never imagining that we need something more than Christ; in Christ God keeps giving us more, so that we can also contemplate in Christ all the experiences and wisdom of the religious traditions around us. Those among us who belong to other traditions or who walk by their own spiritual paths will need to raise up their own words and images for how to be faithful to one's own self and still open to a divine power that is beyond us and yet within all things.

In the end, like the student in the *Crest Jewel* or Arjuna or the Buddha, we have to return to the world that flows ceaselessly around us. Like Kisha Gotami, we must stop clinging to things we used to cherish. Like Andal and Shatakopan, we have to choose to live lives expectant of wisdom, wanting nothing but God. We will have grown wise when we can look without illusion upon our lives and our world and still be mindful enough to welcome the stranger who appears at our gate like Shiva. We cannot stop looking until we have seen and tasted and touched everything, all at once, as if a Goddess were to rise up within us. We will be fully alive when we can live as did Mohandas Gandhi and Mahasweta Devi, unafraid of violence, not yearning for a better time or place, allowing no separation between ourselves and the poorest of the poor. We can keep moving on to other religious encounters too — with other traditions, new wisdoms — and then share our own stories anew, composing a wisdom to live by here and now. If we can do all this, these first encounters with Hindu wisdom will have borne very great fruit indeed.

I cannot resist closing with another song from Rabindranath Tagore's *Gitanjali,* one which I learned when I first lived in Kathmandu:

Thou hast made me known to friends whom I knew not. Thou hast given me seats in homes not my own. Thou hast brought the distant near and made a brother of the stranger.

I am uneasy at heart when I leave my accustomed shelter; I forget that there abides the old in the new, and that there also thou abidest.

Through birth and death, in this world or in others, wherever thou leadest me it is thou, the same, the one companion of my endless life who ever linkest my heart with bonds of joy to the unfamiliar.

When one knows thee, then alien there is none, then no door is shut. Oh, grant me my prayer that I may never lose the bliss of the touch of the one in the play of the many. (*Gitanjali,* 63)

Bibliography

Many books are mentioned in the footnotes to each chapter, but here are just a few of them, to which the reader can turn profitably for further reading:

Antal and Her Path of Love: Poems of a Woman Saint from South India. Trans. Vidya Dehejia. Albany: State University of New York Press, 1990.

The Bhagavad Gita: Krishna's Counsel in Time of War. Trans. Barbara Miller. New York: Bantam Books, 1986.

Gandhi, Mohandas K. *The Story of My Experiments with Truth.* Trans. Mahadev Desai. New York: Dover Publications, 1983.

Hindu Myths. Ed. and trans. Wendy D. O'Flaherty. New York: Penguin Books, 1984.

Imaginary Maps: Three Stories by Mahasweta Devi. Trans. Gayatri Spivak. New York: Routledge, 1995.

The Middle Length Discourses of the Buddha. Trans. Bhikku Nanamoli and Bhikku Bodhi. Boston: Wisdom Publications, 1995.

Saradananda, Swami. *Ramakrishna, The Great Master.* Madras: Sri Ramakrishna Math, 1952.

Saundarya Lahari (The Ocean of Beauty). Ed. and trans. S. S. Sastri and T. R. Srinivasa Ayyangar. Madras, India, and Wheaton, Ill.: Theosophical Publishing House, 1992.

Tagore, Rabindranath. *Gitanjali, Song Offerings.* New York: Macmillan, 1916.

Upanisads. Trans. Patrick Olivelle. Oxford: Oxford University Press, 1996.

Vivekacudamani of Sri Shankaracarya (The Crest Jewel of Discrimination). Trans. Swami Madhavananda. Calcutta: Advaita Ashrama, 1992; in this country, available from the Vedanta Press, Hollywood, Calif.

In addition, for those desiring a more systematic introduction to the Hindu world I recommend:

Flood, Gavin. *An Introduction to Hinduism.* New York: Cambridge University Press, 1996.

Kinsley, David. *Hinduism.* Englewood Cliffs, N.J.: Prentice-Hall, 1982.

Klostermeier, Klaus. *A Survey of Hinduism.* Albany: State University of New York Press, 1996.

As mentioned at the beginning of this book, I have only sampled the richness of India's Hindu traditions. For readers who wish to look farther afield, I recommend beginning with the translation and adaptation of R. K. Narayan, *Ramayana* (New York: Penguin Books, 1972), and *A Touch of Grace: Songs of Kabir,* trans. Linda Hess and Shukdev Singh (Boston: Shambhala Publications, 1994).

Finally, those interested in a more autobiographical approach to the encounter of religions will appreciate Diana Eck, *Encountering God: A Spiritual Journey from Boseman to Banares* (Boston: Beacon Press, 1993). I have written a bit more about my own experience of India in "In Ten Thousand Places, In Every Blade of Grass: Uneventful but True Confessions about Finding God in India, and Here Too," *Studies in Jesuit Spirituality* 28, no. 3 (May 1996), published by the Seminar on Jesuit Spirituality, 3700 West Pine Blvd., St. Louis, MO 63108.

Index

Other Titles in the Faith Meets Faith Series

Toward a Universal Theology of Religion, Leonard Swidler, Editor
The Myth of Christian Uniqueness, John Hick and Paul F. Knitter, Editors
An Asian Theology of Liberation, Aloysius Pieris, S.J.
The Dialogical Imperative, David Lochhead
Love Meets Wisdom, Aloysius Pieris, S.J.
Many Paths, Eugene Hillman, C.S.Sp.
The Silence of God, Raimundo Panikkar
The Challenge of the Scriptures, Groupe de Recherches Islamo-Chrétien
The Meaning of Christ, John Keenan
Hindu-Christian Dialogue, Harold Coward, Editor
The Emptying God, John B. Cobb, Jr., and Christopher Ives, Editors
Christianity through Non-Christian Eyes, Paul J. Griffiths, Editor
Christian Uniqueness Reconsidered, Gavin D'Costa, Editor
Women Speaking, Women Listening, Maura O'Neill
Bursting the Bonds? Leonard Swidler, Lewis John Eron, Lester Dean, and
    Gerard Sloyan, Editors
One Christ — Many Religions, Stanley J. Samartha
The New Universalism, David J. Krieger
Jesus Christ at the Encounter of World Religions, Jacques Dupuis, S.J.
After Patriarchy, Paula M. Cooey, William R. Eakin, and Jay B. McDaniel,
    Editors
An Apology for Apologetics, Paul J. Griffiths
World Religions and Human Liberation, Dan Cohn-Sherbok, Editor
Uniqueness, Gabriel Moran
Leave the Temple, Felix Wilfred, Editor
The Buddha and the Christ, Leo D. Lefebure
The Divine Matrix, Joseph A. Bracken, S.J.
The Gospel of Mark: A Mahāyāna Reading, John P. Keenan
Salvations, S. Mark Heim
The Intercultural Challenge of Raimon Panikkar, Joseph Prabhu, Editor
*Fire and Water: Women, Society, and Spirituality in Buddhism and Chris-
    tianity,* Aloysius Pieris, S.J.
Piety and Power: Muslims and Christians in West Africa, Lamin Sanneh
Life after Death in World Religions, Harold Coward, Editor
The Uniqueness of Jesus, Paul Mojzes and Leonard Swidler, Editors
A Pilgrim in Chinese Culture, Judith A. Berling
West African Religious Traditions, Robert B. Fisher, S.V.D.